Assassination A HISTORY OF POLITICAL MURDER

Assassination

A HISTORY OF POLITICAL MURDER

Lindsay Porter

With 152 illustrations, 78 in colour

Frontispiece: *Detail of a 15th-century woodcut depicting the assassination of Julius Caesar (see p. 10).*

Illustration on p. 192: *Bomb made by anarchists in Barcelona, 1908.*

First published in the United Kingdom in 2010 by
Thames & Hudson Ltd, 181A High Holborn,
London WC1V 7QX

thamesandhudson.com

British Library Cataloguing-in-Publication Data
A catalogue record for this book is available from the
British Library

ISBN 978-0-500-25158-4

Printed and bound in China by Hung Hing Offset Printing
Company Ltd

Contents

Introduction: *Assassins and 'Hashishin'*

Assassination has never changed the history of the world.

– Benjamin Disraeli[1]

The 19th-century prime minister Disraeli made this surprising assertion as he addressed Parliament in 1865, following the murder of Abraham Lincoln by John Wilkes Booth – the first of what would become a long sequence of presidential assassinations and assassination attempts. Making no reference to the political issues that were then dividing the North and South of the United States, the British prime minister instead paid tribute to Lincoln the man, whose final hours were 'homely' and 'innocent', rather than to Lincoln the statesman. In so doing, he highlighted the flaw at the heart of assassination plots throughout history: the conflation of the individual with the state they represent. Disraeli went on to mention 'the costly sacrifice of a Caesar', and 'the violent deaths' of the French king Henri IV and the Dutch prince William the Silent. None of these murders, he attested, changed the course of history; none stopped 'the inevitable destiny of his country'.

And yet assassination has been used as a political tool since the earliest times. The food-tasters at the courts of old may have been replaced by secret servicemen and armed bodyguards, but the peril inherent in being a head of state has not gone away. From the removal of tyrants in Classical civilization to the state-sanctioned 'decapitation strikes' of the present day, assassination remains a political tactic, even if the methods and the motivations may have changed. The concept of the assassin, too, has undergone various permutations. Assassins have been feared and revered in equal measure, and their popular image has shifted from principled political actor and revolutionary to unhinged anarchist, hitman and religious fanatic. They appear motivated by political conviction, the desire to change history, a hunger for power and money or simply by a longing for fame.

The modern idea of the assassin – the cold, ruthless, professional killer – has its roots in an 11th-century Ismaili Muslim sect, the 'Hashishin', which operated in the Middle East from 1090 to 1272. In the popular imagination these warriors were the terror of the Crusades,

The 44-calibre Deringer used to shoot Abraham Lincoln. Lincoln's assassination continues to fascinate: the 16th president of the United States was the first to be assassinated, and the details surrounding his murder, including the bizarre afterlife of his killer's corpse, contributed to what has been described as America's longest-running conspiracy theory.

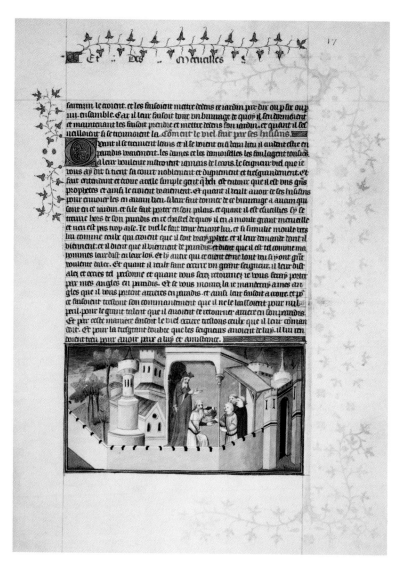

above The most exotic legends surrounding the origins of assassination go back to Marco Polo in the 13th century, but they have no support in any authentic Eastern source. This portrait of Marco Polo is from the 1477 edition of his Travels.

right Marco Polo's story is repeated in the early 15th-century Livre des merveilles du monde. This miniature shows Hassan-i Sabbah initiating his followers into the ways of the Hashishin. According to legend, he drugged these warriors at his castle at Alamut (today in northern Iran), and tempted them with all manner of earthly pleasures to ensure their lasting loyalty.

committing random acts of killing; but in reality their deeds were politically motivated, and directed more towards Muslim rulers than the Crusaders. It was Marco Polo who first described their alleged exploits, which for the Western imagination presented an irresistible combination of drugs, sex and death. In his *Travels*, probably written at the end of the 13th century, Marco Polo relates the legend of the Hashishin's founder, Hassan-i Sabbah ('the Old Man of the Mountain'), and how he supposedly trained his assassins in the castle of Alamut, perched high in the Alborz mountains in what is now northern Iran. The recruits would be drugged and brought to the castle, where they would wake in its garden, 'the largest … and most beautiful that was ever seen'. In the garden lived 'ladies and the most beautiful damsels', whose purpose was 'to furnish the young men … with all delights and pleasures'. Believing they had woken in Paradise (so the legend goes), these youths were prepared to do anything their leader demanded – even leaping from the castle walls into the ravine below – provided they were allowed to return there. The recruits were then trained to kill with silent, deadly expertise. Their modus operandi was to attack in public places before melting undetected into the crowd, leaving behind scenes of fear and confusion. They might assert their superiority by placing a dagger on the pillow of a powerful enemy, in order to prove how a target of the Hashishin was not safe, even within his own heavily protected walls.

The legacy of these early assassins lives on in the popular imagination – the ruthlessness, the need to inspire fear, the almost supernatural ability to avoid detection – and resurfaced in the mythical brainwashed killers of the cold war. The early assassins have perhaps more in common than we might think with the men who stabbed Julius Caesar to death in 44 BC, in that they were essentially political killers.

A 19th-century interpretation of the assassination of Prince William of Orange ('the Silent') in Delft on 10 July 1584. For twelve years William had led the revolt of the Netherlands against Philip II of Spain, but his murder by the Catholic Balthasar Gérard deprived the movement of a leader. William the Silent holds the dubious distinction of being the first head of state to be killed with a handgun.

Harmodius and Aristogeiton, later known as the 'Tyrannicides', became symbols of Athenian democracy for plotting against the unpopular rulers Hippias and Hipparchus in the late 6th century BC.

Whether Caesar's murder was the expression of a democratic revolt against dictatorship or the result of factional infighting among the aristocracy, its significance as a possible political process took hold in the ancient world. Subsequent cultures, too, appropriated and reinvented the concept, so that the figure of Brutus, for example, was evoked by later assassins as a symbol of the righteous tyrannicide.

Julius Caesar's assassination provides the template for the philosophical and political debates that have surrounded political murder in the Western world ever since.

According to Plutarch, who was writing a century and a half after the event, Brutus justified the killing of Caesar by describing him as a dictator, putting aside his personal affection for the man and viewing him solely in his relation to the state: the tyrant who must be removed to safeguard Rome as a republic. The justification for political murder – in this case tyrannicide – has been repeatedly explored, debated and reinterpreted throughout history, and continues to be so today. Arguably, the covert assassination plots devised by the CIA during the cold war can be seen as a continuation of the ancient Greeks' argument that removing a despot was justified. What is open to interpretation, of course, is what counts as despotic rule, and – to use the example of America's decades-long anti-Castro programme – how much that definition is influenced by the opponent's ideology.

During the Middle Ages, the debate surrounding tyrannicide was joined by theologians, who reinterpreted

A Mughal manuscript of c. 1528 depicting the murder of King Chosroes II of Persia in 628 while under house arrest. According to Muslim lore, his death had been foretold by the Prophet.

Classical ideas about tyrannical rule to include questions of faith. The philosophers of ancient Greece would have recognized John of Salisbury's statement, made in the middle of the 12th century, that 'Between a tyrant and a prince there is this single or chief difference, that the latter obeys the law.'[2] But John of Salisbury and his peers equated disregard for the law of the land with disregard for the law of God. The tyrant was no longer simply guilty of what the ancients described as 'whim and passion': he was guilty of the crime of heresy, which was punishable by death. Both Henri III and Henri IV of France were assassinated by religious fanatics convinced of their monarchs' heresy. Henri IV's Huguenot upbringing meant that he was the target of assassins for most of his life, surviving several attempts before succumbing to François Ravaillac's blade in 1610. Ravaillac was never part of a larger political conspiracy, but he was clearly influenced by the atmosphere of intolerance generated by the Wars of Religion that raged at the time. During the 18th century philosophers again looked to the ancients for inspiration, bypassing religion in a bid to discard what they perceived as the superstitions of the previous centuries. Classical notions of virtue and sacrifice, as personified by the noble regicide Brutus, contributed to Charlotte Corday's decision to assassinate the French revolutionary Jean-Paul Marat.

It is not unusual for the victim's reputation to undergo a radical transformation after death. Thomas Becket, previously the worldly and cantankerous archbishop of Canterbury, was even sanctified; but there are others who become secular saints, their characters polished and honed almost beyond recognition. Jean-Paul Marat became – at least for as long as the Jacobin government lasted – a martyr of the French revolution, a secular icon to replace the Christian saints that had been destroyed in the making of the new republic. Pancho Villa and Emiliano Zapata, hunted and killed by their own government during the Mexican revolution, metamorphosed over time into symbols of Mexico itself, appropriated by subsequent governments regardless of their political affiliation. Towering above all these is the figure of President John F. Kennedy, whose assassination, and the netherworld of conspiracy theories that now surrounds it, makes it almost impossible to assess his achievements with any kind of objectivity.

By the 19th century the assassin's methods and motives had taken a turn that we can – unfortunately – recognize today. Previously, the assassin and victim had always been in close proximity, and the assassin was inevitably caught. With the invention of dynamite, however, the assassin no longer even had to be present at the time of the murder

Spencer Perceval is the only British prime minister to have died by assassination – a cruel fate made even crueller by the fact that this is virtually his only claim to fame. He was shot by a bankrupt Liverpool stockbroker, who blamed Perceval for his losses, on 11 May 1812 as he entered the lobby of the House of Commons. The prime minister died almost instantly. This illustration is from the Newgate Calendar, *a popular publication depicting the lives and deeds of notorious criminals.*

A hand reaches out of the crowd and fires a pistol at Pope John Paul II on 13 May 1981 (top left). Miraculously, he survived. The gunman, Mehmet Ali Agca (bottom right), has never given a convincing reason for the attack (at the time, the US government even suspected Soviet involvement), but it seems to have been politically, rather than religiously, motivated.

(but neither could he or she predict who might be caught in the explosion). Victims were now chosen for what they represented rather than for what they did. Bosnian nationalists targeted Archduke Franz Ferdinand as a symbol of the Habsburg dynasty, not because of any policies specific to him. Anarchist assassins trained their sights on individuals, then institutions, then symbols of the bourgeois society they were trying to overthrow, until violence became an end in itself. The age of modern terrorism had begun.

Assassination looks at key episodes throughout history, from the assassination of Julius Caesar to the targeted terrorism central to many of today's nationalist and fundamentalist struggles. It examines the assassins' actions and the rationale that underpinned them in order to gauge how ideas about political murder have changed over time. Finally, it places each assassination in a wider context, looking at its aftermath and considering whether, ultimately, Disraeli was correct.

chapter 1

Plotting the Ancient World:
Julius Caesar

A tall, fair-skinned man, borne on a litter and dressed in the purple robes that only he was entitled to wear, arrived at the Theatre of Pompey to attend a meeting with his senators. A familiar figure – a soothsayer he had met some days earlier – caught his eye, and Caesar paused his retinue. He said, triumphantly, 'The Ides of March have come.' The figure considered, before replying, 'Yes, but they have not passed.'[1]

Inside, a crowd surged around the great man. Petitions were thrust forward, and there were requests for an audience, appeals for clemency for relatives. One of the senators, Lucius Tullius Cimber, put forward a plea on behalf of his brother in exile – a terrible fate for any Roman – and others joined his entreaty. The dictator rejected their requests with a dismissive wave, but they became insistent, jostling and crowding against him, until he was forced to push violently against the encroaching mass. Tullius tore the robes from Caesar's shoulders and, as though following a signal, the tribune Casca drew his dagger and plunged it into Caesar's neck. At this, the surrounding men each stabbed him, even wounding one another in their haste. Fighting his way through the attackers, Caesar caught sight of his trusted praetor and confidant Marcus Junius Brutus, who stood among the conspirators with dagger drawn. A moment of recognition – a horrible realization – and Caesar pulled his robe over his head, resigned to the blows raining down on him. There were twenty-three wounds in all, one for each of the conspirators.

The assassination of Julius Caesar in 44 BC, carried out by a conspiracy of his closest political advisors and friends, has haunted the Western imagination from the moment it occurred. It provoked questions that have exercised philosophers, historians, politicians and revolutionaries for two thousand years: Can tyrannicide be justified, and how does one define 'tyrant'? What is the nature of public versus private duty? And should violence be used as a political tool? The way in which the deed and its protagonists have been interpreted and reinterpreted in different periods – variously championed or maligned – tells us a great deal about the morals, ideals and political concerns of each epoch. Caesar has at various times been viewed as tyrant or martyr, and Brutus as a villain or self-sacrificing hero. As the character of one is re-evaluated,

The assassination of Julius Caesar on the Ides of March, 44 BC, is the most famous political murder in history. This early 19th-century reconstruction, by Friedrich Heinrich Füger, mirrors the account given by Plutarch, in which Casca struck the first blow.

Caesar's defeat of his great rival Pompey at the Battle of Pharsalus (48 BC) was among his military triumphs. He did not, however, forget their earlier friendship, and when he arrived in Alexandria to find that Pompey had been murdered, he is said to have wept bitter tears, turning away from the man who brought him Pompey's head 'with loathing, as from an assassin'. Painting by Giovanni Antonio Pellegrini, c. 1724–25.

so the other is cast in a new light. Shakespeare was clearly aware of this symbiotic relationship, giving the two figures equal prominence in his drama.

The Classical world has left us several accounts of the assassination. If the version in Plutarch's *Lives*, written in the early 2nd century AD, is perhaps the best known today, that is largely because Shakespeare used it as source material for his play. Plutarch was writing some 150 years after the event, however. The orator Cicero, who was politically active at the time of Caesar's death, is strangely silent concerning the assassination itself, but does write at length about the philosophical issues that would have concerned Caesar's killers. The histories of Suetonius (*Lives of the Caesars*, written AD 121), Appian (*Roman History*, before c. AD 165) and Cassius Dio (*Roman History*, before AD 229) also discuss Caesar's death; although there are some variations in detail, there is enough consensus to create a clear picture of the assassination, the events leading up to it, and its effect on the instigators and on the Roman people as a whole.

Julius Caesar (100–44 BC) had brought a period of stability – albeit short-lived – to a state that had suffered nearly a century of turmoil. During that time Rome had seen murder, civil war and Spartacus' slave uprising – a situation that inspired one visitor to describe it as 'a city for sale and waiting for destruction if it but find a buyer'.[2] An ever-widening gulf between rich and poor had created a society simmering with unease, paranoid on the one hand, resentful on the other. This was the Rome in which Caesar had begun his career. Although his patrician background might have suggested otherwise, Caesar aligned himself politically with the democratic rather than the aristocratic party. He was a brilliant strategist on the battlefield, and proved himself equally adept in political life. An early reputation for oratory preceded a steady climb up the ladder of public office. In 60 BC, he set his sights on winning the consulship despite the objections of some in the Senate, and devised a great alliance with Marcus Licinius Crassus and Pompey (the First Triumvirate) that dominated Rome for seven years. At the same time Caesar led a conquest of Gaul, extending Roman power as far as northern France. The death of Crassus in 53 BC, however, led to the collapse of the coalition, and Caesar's relations with Pompey became hostile. With Caesar still in Gaul, the Senate, fearing the support he enjoyed among the people, demanded that Caesar should give up his command; he refused as long as Pompey kept an army, and was thereafter declared an enemy of the people. With his crossing of the Rubicon into Italy in 49 BC, civil war broke out.

Caesar pursued Pompey through Italy and into Greece, where he dealt a final blow to his erstwhile ally at the Battle of Pharsalus in 48 BC. On his return to Rome he was named dictator – an office normally reserved for times of national crisis – and then, two years later, was made dictator for a period of ten years. Under Caesar's rule, the city enjoyed a measure of peace and prosperity, its people benefiting from an ambitious series of public improvements and entertainments. Suetonius, for example, writes of the extravagant public displays and celebrations organized by Caesar following his military successes in Egypt and Africa, where he had routed Pompey's followers. These festivities included a banquet for 22,000 guests, gladiatorial combats and commemorative pageants celebrating victories at sea. Caesar also instigated a series of lavish building projects: a new Senate House and Forum, for instance, and the expansion of the Circus Maximus to accommodate 150,000 spectators and a new moat to drain the racetrack. Such displays of largesse trumpeted Rome's status to the rest of the world and at the same time secured the people's affection for their dictator.

Publicly, Caesar's successful military campaigns and ambitious building projects inspired admiration. Yet such achievements could not mask a character that was (his contemporaries believed) complex to the point of paradox. On the one hand, he was respected for his courage and relentless energy, and was widely recognized as a skilful orator and a cunning military strategist. He was known to be moderate in his diet, revealing a self-control and temperance quite at odds with contemporary levels of gluttony among the wealthy. Accounts of fits or fainting spells suggest that he may have been epileptic, yet his ability to overcome any apparent physical infirmities earned him the sympathy and respect of his peers. Stories of Caesar's generosity were legion: he was known to be kind to his soldiers and his many friends, and frequently displayed great

Andrea Mantegna, The Triumphs of Caesar, *1490s. This series of nine canvases was painted for the powerful Gonzaga family, rulers of Mantua in northern Italy, who viewed Caesar as a symbol of military glory. In evoking these spoils and trophies, Mantegna drew on Classical accounts of Roman triumphs.*

Julius Caesar wearing the laurel crown, from a manuscript of Plutarch's Lives, c. 1450.

clemency to his enemies (those who were Romans, at any rate). And yet he possessed a widely recognized ruthlessness of character. For all his generosity, he was also known to be conniving, lustful and cruel. If Classical historians found it difficult to reconcile these apparently contradictory aspects of Caesar's personality, there was one on which they were all agreed: his overriding ambition. If it spurred him to greater achievements than his predecessors, it might also have led to his downfall.

Following Caesar's triumphant return from his Spanish campaigns in 44 BC, he was awarded the title of 'perpetual dictator' – that is to say, dictator for life rather than for a renewable one-year term. Despite this unprecedented honour, he continued to display signs of magnanimity and clemency, bestowing favours according to merit and granting pardons to his enemies. But the senators were becoming wary. Was Caesar's hunger for power the sign of a future tyrant? What were the implications for Rome if his ambition were allowed full rein?

Despite the reservations some may have had concerning Caesar's growing power, others appeared to be falling over themselves to devise yet more honours for their leader, their extravagant displays of sycophancy effectively reinforcing his critics' fears. In the months leading up to Caesar's appointment as dictator for life, his birthday was declared a public holiday and his birth month was renamed Julius.

Statues in his likeness began to appear throughout Italy and were erected in every Roman temple. In late 45 or early 44 Caesar started to wear a golden crown of laurel leaves, the symbol of the early Etruscan kings. In quick succession he adopted the purple robes worn by rulers of the past, was provided with a gold throne in the Senate, had a shrine dedicated to him, and was accorded the rare right to be buried within the walls of the city. This frenzy for contriving and bestowing honours could be a means either of currying favour with the dictator or of undermining him. It seems that all this flattery might have led to a stunning breach of protocol on Caesar's part when, on one occasion, he refused to rise to greet the senators coming to address him. Even he realized the error of such disrespect, explaining it away by saying that he had been unwell. But there was one symbol that he did refuse to adopt: the title of 'king'.

For the ancient Romans, *Rex* was a heavily weighted term, evoking the despotic reign of the last kings of Rome; the Tarquins had been driven from the city in 510 BC by Lucius Junius Brutus, one of Marcus Junius Brutus's ancestors. The very idea of monarchy was anathema to the Roman people: it was on the rejection of monarchy that the republic had been founded, and Caesar's contemporaries viewed themselves as continuing in that tradition. For the ancient sources, two events stand out that, rightly or wrongly, linked Caesar with the kingship. Plutarch describes how Caesar, on being first addressed as 'Rex' by a vociferous crowd, corrected them with a dismissive 'the name is Caesar'. This has been seen, variously, as concrete proof of his rejection of kingship or, conversely, as a display of arrogance and an illustration of his perceived superiority even over that exalted rank. According to Cicero, a few days after Caesar had accepted the title of perpetual dictator, and as the feast of the Lupercalia was being celebrated, he was offered the title of *Rex* again, this time in the form of a diadem that Mark Antony attempted to place on his head. Again, both the action and the rejection are ambiguous in meaning. Some historians saw it as a way for Caesar's supporters to demonstrate publicly the limits of his ambitions: despite the proliferation of honours being pressed upon him, by rejecting the title of *Rex* he was sending a clear message that his political aspirations were not at odds with the principles on which the republic was founded. Others, however, interpreted the offer as a way for his enemies to test him, since public acceptance of the title would reveal the extent of his hubris and damage his popular following. A third theory suggests that Caesar himself wanted to test the public's reaction, to gauge whether they could accept the notion of kingship. All illustrate different sides of the debate that surrounded Caesar's power and political ambitions.

Suspicion of monarchy was part of Brutus's
family history. When one of his ancestors,
Lucius Junius Brutus, discovered that his
own sons were conspiring to restore the hated
Tarquins, he had them executed for the good
of the Roman Republic. In 1789 Jacques-
Louis David depicted the sons' bodies being
brought home. The image's message of
stoical self-sacrifice for the good of the state
would not have been lost during the time of
the French revolution.

above *Bust of Gaius Cassius Longinus,
one of the conspirators in Caesar's
assassination. Cassius came to be
viewed as Brutus's opposite, motivated
by the personal animosity he felt towards
the dictator rather than concern for
the republic.*

below *Cicero, the great statesman,
philosopher and orator. In the months
following Caesar's assassination,
he considered the nature of tyrannicide
in his work* On Duties.

Whatever the true meaning behind these two events, the
connection had been made. As perpetual dictator, was Caesar essentially
just a king by another name? It seems that his powers, his titles and his
control of political offices were unpalatable to many – even those who
belonged to his own party.

Among other philosophical questions, Cicero addressed the
nature of tyranny and the dangers of unchecked ambition in his
philosophical treatise *On Duties;* devised in the form a letter to his son,
it was written in the months that followed Caesar's assassination. In it,
Cicero draws parallels between Rome's founder, Romulus, and Caesar's
quest for power. Romulus murdered his brother, Remus, in order to
reign alone, and in so doing 'he threw to the winds his brotherly
affection and his human feelings'.[3] Cicero accuses Caesar of similar
crimes in the name of self-interest and the pursuit of power, illustrating
that his position as dictator had come about through his rivalry with,
and ultimate destruction of, Pompey during the civil war. This anecdote
allowed Cicero to voice the potential dangers of political ambition
carried to its ultimate conclusion while making allusions to historical
precedent. And his concerns were not unique: as Caesar's power increased,
those of his senators were in danger of being curtailed, with potentially
disastrous consequences for Rome as a republic. A group of senators, led
by Brutus and Gaius Cassius Longinus, began to conspire against their
dictator perpetuo and held a series of secret meetings in one another's houses
in which the idea of his assassination emerged. After several proposals
were discussed and rejected, it was at last agreed that a Senate meeting
would provide the best opportunity. Since they were all senators, the
conspirators could gather in large numbers without arousing suspicion;
and once the deed was done, they would have the attention of the rest of
the Senate, allowing them to explain their cause. The old Senate House
had burned down eight years earlier, so business had temporarily moved
to an anteroom of the Theatre of Pompey (originally situated in what is
now the Largo di Torre Argentina). The next meeting would take place
around the middle – or the Ides – of March.

The Roman political elite operated in an incredibly small world:
Brutus and Cassius were brothers-in-law, and Pompey, Caesar's erstwhile
adversary, had killed Brutus's father. Brutus's mother was one of Caesar's
favourite mistresses, leading to (somewhat unlikely) rumours that
Caesar was his father. The question of personal sacrifice for the public
good was thus also a personal matter, since Caesar's peers were also his
kinsmen. It is precisely because of the unnaturalness of the murder –
the transgression against the sanctity of kinship – that Brutus becomes

Edward Poynter's The Ides of March, *painted in 1883. Poynter looked to Shakespeare rather than to earlier sources for this theatrical work. Here, Calpurnia gestures to the comet she interprets as a sign for Caesar to stay away from the Senate the following day.*

ennobled, both in Plutarch's telling of his life and in Shakespeare's play; his personal connection with Caesar makes him more than an assassin, but also 'the noblest Roman' on account of the personal sacrifice he is prepared to make for the good of his countrymen. Plutarch emphasizes how Brutus has no personal quarrel with Caesar and is motivated purely by the abstract ideal of removing a tyrant from the body politic. Classical historians are keen to point out the strength of Brutus's character and the esteem in which he was held by his peers. Indeed, it is a sign of the respect he commanded that he was able to win over so many of the senators to his cause: as Plutarch states, they all agreed as long as 'Brutus took the lead, arguing that the undertaking demanded … the reputation of a man like him'.[4] We are told that Cassius, by contrast, felt a personal animosity against Caesar: 'Brutus, it is said, objected to the rule, but Cassius hated the ruler.'[5] The meaning is clear: Cassius was a cold-blooded killer, taking advantage of the political situation to act on personal grievances.

The days leading up to the assassination were marked by a series of portents. Brutus, although publicly resolved to carry out the deed and convinced of its necessity, was privately troubled, his sleep broken. His wife, Porcia, was able to convince him to share the reason for his distress only after she had proven her courage by plunging a dagger into her thigh. Once told of the plot, she spent the day of the assassination in a highly agitated state, demanding news from the Senate from every passer-by.

In spite of the conspirators' secrecy, rumours began to reach those close to Caesar, who warned him against visiting the Senate on the

According to Plutarch, Porcia proved her bravery and capacity for discretion to Brutus by stabbing her thigh with a knife. This work, painted by Ercole de' Roberti in c. 1486–90, is one of a series depicting women from Classical antiquity who displayed acts of heroism.

inauspicious day. This advice was seconded by his doctors, who were alarmed by what may have been an attack of epilepsy (described by ancient historians as the 'falling sickness'). Caesar's wife, Calpurnia, had been troubled by nightmares, having dreamt the previous night that she had cradled her dead husband in her arms, and tried to prevent him from going. When Caesar tried to postpone the meeting, his trusted lieutenant Decimus Brutus – who was party to the conspiracy – persuaded him to attend, dismissing his concerns as 'women's dreams and the gossip of idle men'. Plutarch emphasizes the fateful nature of the episode ('destiny, it would seem, is not so much unexpected as unavoidable') – as if all the participants were merely acting out the parts allocated to them – and tells of unexplained crashing sounds, lights in the sky, birds swooping into the Forum and legions of men in flames. Most troubling of all is his account of the sacrifice Caesar made before meeting the Senate. It was customary to read the entrails of a slain animal as a form of prophesy; when Caesar's sacrifice was cut open, it was revealed to have no heart.

Despite these portents and the soothsayer's ominous utterances, Caesar arrived at the Senate meeting as planned; according to Plutarch, it was as though 'some heavenly power seemed to be conducting Caesar to Pompey's vengeance'. All the senators rose in his honour, but then the conspirators closed in until, 'hemmed in on all sides … driven hither and thither like a wild beast [he] was entangled in the hands of all'.[6] When they had finished, Caesar lay dead at the foot of a statue of Pompey.

Following the assassination, all was confusion: many of the conspirators, Brutus included, had been wounded in the mêlée, and the assembled witnesses recoiled in horror at the spectacle before them. The assassins burst from the Senate, the sight of the bloodied mob causing panic in the streets. Doors were bolted, shutters slammed and locked, and shops and counters were left unattended as people ran to and fro, spreading the news. The accounts of what happened next vary; some historians claim that the conspirators were forced to flee to the Capitol for their own safety, but Plutarch describes a more stirring scene. When it appeared that the violence had subsided, a crowd followed Brutus as he and a handful of conspirators headed for the Capitol, still brandishing their bloody daggers – 'not like fugitives, but with glad faces and full of confidence'.[7] There Brutus announced the death of Caesar and attempted to win over a terrified public by exhorting them to reclaim their republic from the threat of tyranny. As senators, the conspirators had sworn allegiance to their dictator; they had been duty-bound to protect him.

Jean-Léon Gérôme's painting (1867; detail) represents Caesar's assassination as a turning point in world history. The successful conspirators, the deed done, seem almost to be participating in some solemn ritual.

Brutus defended his breaking of the oath by claiming that no one could bind a Roman to a tyrant, and that his first duty was to Rome itself. Caesar's personal ambitions, he implied, had affected his ability to rule justly; and since Caesar was no longer fulfilling his duties as ruler, his senators were exempt from fulfilling theirs. Brutus's defence of tyrannicide, and questions concerning the respective duties of monarch and subject and their relation to each other, would preoccupy future philosophers and theologians throughout the Western world.

In the aftermath of the murder, it looked as though Brutus's character would win over public opinion; loyalty to the slain leader was initially outweighed by the deep respect in which Brutus was held by his peers. The public's apparent acceptance of the deed, however, led the senators to make some errors of judgment. The conspirators had initially planned to throw Caesar's body unceremoniously into the Tiber. But Mark Antony, Caesar's deputy, insisted on a full public funeral, which together with the reading of Caesar's will – which bequeathed three pieces of gold to each Roman citizen – won back public sympathy for Caesar. The sight of his mutilated body, carried with full pomp and divine honours through the Forum, enflamed the crowd; they ransacked nearby streets for wooden railings, tables and benches, which they heaped round the body and set on fire. Then, in a frenzy, they ran with flaming torches to the homes of the conspirators, intent on killing them. Brutus and his associates escaped mob justice, but one man named Cinna – a friend of Caesar's who had gone to the Forum out of respect – was mistaken for a conspirator of the same name and torn to pieces. For their own safety, Brutus and Cassius left Rome soon after.

Caesar's funeral was an elaborate affair arranged by Mark Antony. His body would have been carried in procession, attended by musicians and mourners – as in this relief from a contemporary sarcophagus.

Politically, the outcome of Caesar's assassination was a shambles. His assassins had no plan to restore Rome beyond removing Caesar himself. Their mistake was in not going far enough: Cassius had pushed for the assassination of Mark Antony as well, but Brutus had faith that the machinery of the republic would somehow reassert itself once the corrupting influence of the tyrant had been eradicated. He was wrong: Caesar's death was the beginning of a period of civil war, after which Mark Antony, Octavian (later Augustus Caesar) and Marcus Aemilius Lepidus emerged as rulers under the Second Triumvirate. This legally sanctioned political alliance would remain in power until 33 BC. Cicero, who was sympathetic to the conspirators' cause, bemoaned their failure to restore the republic, writing to his friend Atticus, 'Good god, the tyranny survives though the tyrant is dead!'[8] The seven emperors who succeeded Augustus all suffered violent deaths (or were rumoured to have done so), either by assassination or as victims of suicide. After Caesar's murder, tyrannicide became what one historian described as 'part of the new order of things'[9] – almost a legitimate way of attempting to change a regime.

In Western culture, Caesar's assassination cast a long shadow. Many of the Classical accounts suggest that it was unavoidable, 'among events of divine ordering'.[10] Plutarch mentions not only the portents and visions that preceded the deed, but also the omens that followed it: a comet showed in the sky for seven days after Caesar's death, and the sun shone feebly for a whole year, leading to crop failures. And although this view implies that those who participated in the tragedy were somehow destined to play their part, they do not escape censure: the greatest hint that they somehow displeased the gods comes in Plutarch, where Brutus is visited by the spirit of his 'evil genius' (which Shakespeare turned into Caesar's ghost). Plutarch could not bring himself to condemn Brutus, however, blaming the crime rather than the criminal. He was writing at a time when republican virtue was held in high regard, and Brutus was viewed as its noble embodiment.

The ancient Greeks (to whom we owe the word 'tyrant') were agreed that tyrannicide was not a crime. 'Great is the honour bestowed not on him who kills a thief, but on him who kills a tyrant,'[11] Plato declared. Both he and Aristotle had used the term to mean a monarch who rules according to whim rather than the law, favouring the personal over the public good. Plato in particular introduced a moral dimension, equating tyranny with degeneracy, injustice and despotism in a way that earlier Greek writers would not have recognized. Roman authors seemed to share this view, and they were united in their admiration for Lucius

Junius Brutus, Marcus Brutus's ancestor, who as part of his campaign to rid Rome of the despotic Tarquin kings had killed his own sons for conspiring with them. For later writers, he served as the model of one who sacrifices personal feelings for the good of the state; it is clear that Plutarch (and, later, Shakespeare) had him in mind when they wrote their accounts of Marcus Brutus. (Cassius they both regarded as Brutus's moral counterweight – a man who held a grudge against Caesar the individual as well as Caesar the leader).

Caesar's assassination proved to be the ideal case study for exploring ideas surrounding the nature of tyranny and, by extension, the duties of the monarch to his or her subjects, and vice versa. The term 'tyrant' itself continued to carry different connotations throughout history, referring sometimes to the manner in which the ruler acquired power (by usurpation, for example, in which case the concept is called *tyrannus in titula*), and sometimes to the way in which the ruler exerted power (by oppression, for instance, when it is known as *tyrannus in regimine*).

In the post-Classical period, as the principle of hereditary kingship and monarchical legitimacy became more important, theologians too began to address the definition of tyranny and the justification for tyrannicide. One idea that seemed especially pertinent was the theory that a monarch might be accused of tyranny if his right to the throne were in question, regardless of the nature of his rule. These debates still incorporated the two issues that had been raised by the writers of antiquity – the legitimacy of the ruler and the legality or morality of his rule – but they were now addressed in relation to the church. For instance, St Augustine, writing in the 5th century, urged resistance

Caesar's assassination did not, of course, remove the threat of tyranny; on the contrary, it made it inevitable. His nephew and heir, Octavian, proclaimed himself emperor in 27 BC, bringing the Roman Republic to a close. This famous cameo, of c. AD 23 , shows Augustus himself (top left); his son-in-law, Tiberius (centre, enthroned); and Caligula, the third Roman emperor, as a small boy (far left).

Tullius Servius (d. 535 BC), the sixth legendary king of Rome, is said to have been assassinated by his own daughter and her husband, Tarquinius Superbus. Livy alleges that his daughter drove a chariot over his dying body. The rights and wrongs of killing tyrants became a much debated topic of political morality.

In 1407 Louis I of Orléans was murdered on the orders of the duke of Burgundy. Jean Petit, a Franciscan theologian, defended the act on the grounds that he had been a tyrant, but it was condemned by the Council of Constance eight years later. The debate continued, and may well have influenced the killing of Henri IV in 1610.

against the ruler who acts contrary to the laws of God, but insisted that the monarch who acts contrary to the laws of man must be obeyed, no matter how unjust his rule. The role of the monarch in determining the definition of tyranny was also debated, principally by John of Salisbury (Thomas Becket's clerk) in the 12th century and Thomas Aquinas in the 13th century. Taking their lead from the Classical philosophers, they both concluded that tyrannical rule was defined by behaviour that went against the good of the community. Injustice, be it defined in relation to the law of the land or the law of God, could be resisted legitimately, even to the extent of committing regicide. These two interpretations – tyranny as defined by God, or tyranny as defined by the law or the community – remained central to the debate, with the balance tipping first one way, then the other over time. The brutal murder of Louis I of Orléans by the duke of Burgundy in 1407, which had been defended on the grounds of tyranny by the Franciscan theologian Jean Petit, led the church to condemn tyrannicide unequivocally at the Council

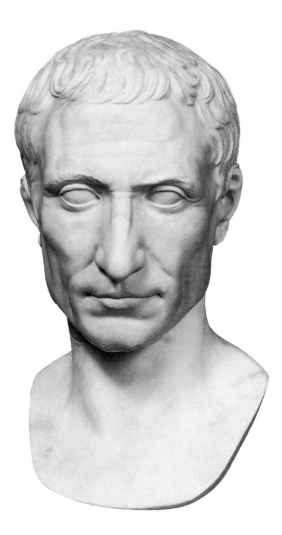

After his death, Caesar was idealized. His features were adapted to Greek conventions of portraiture, designed to convey intelligence and authority.

of Constance in 1415. Theologians would uphold this view until the Spanish Jesuit Juan de Mariana revisited the question in his treatise *De rege et regis institutione* ('On the King and the Institution of Kingship') of 1599, once again making a claim for the justification of tyrannicide. Many believed that Mariana might have influenced Henri IV's assassin, the religious fanatic Ravaillac, albeit indirectly. The king's murder in 1610 led Pope Paul V to renew the decree of the Council of Constance in a papal bull of 24 January 1615. Mariana's book was publicly burnt, and the Jesuits were expelled from Paris.

It was during the Renaissance that the story of Caesar's assassination entered the cultural sphere. No longer was the issue of tyrannicide limited to the realms of philosophy; it was now reinterpreted on a human level, through the characters who had been involved in the fateful deed. In the 14th century Dante placed Brutus in the last circle of hell, with Judas Iscariot and Satan for company, but by the 16th century his character – like that of the other main players – allowed writers and artists to put a human face to abstract themes such as the nature of duty, sacrifice and nobility – most notably explored in Shakespeare's play *Julius Caesar*, written around 1599. The complexities of Brutus's personality and the ambiguities of his situation are so fully explored that many began to see Brutus as the real tragic hero of the piece. The duke of Buckingham made this explicit when he wrote a drama in two parts – *The Tragedy of Julius Caesar* and *The Tragedy of Brutus* – in 1722.

From the late 18th century Brutus became a shorthand for republican virtue. In the town halls and public squares of revolutionary France, the bust of his ancestor Lucius Junius Brutus appeared alongside the female allegorical figure of Liberty. Yet the endless mutability of Marcus Brutus as a symbol continued, so that even the monarchist Charlotte Corday evoked his name at her trial for the assassination of the Jacobin revolutionary Jean-Paul Marat. Her willingness to sacrifice her own life for the good of her country, and her reported composure at her execution in 1793, won over even hardened republicans. In the 19th century Abraham Lincoln's assassin, John Wilkes Booth, likened himself to Brutus in his aim to free America from what he perceived as the tyranny of Lincoln's administration; he seemed genuinely perplexed that the American people did not share his view of the president as a tyrant and of himself as a liberator. For twelve days, wounded and on the run, he evaded capture, until he was killed by cavalry officers in a farmhouse where he had taken refuge, in April 1865.

Silver denarius commemorating the death of Caesar, with a profile of Brutus on one side, and the cap of liberty flanked by daggers on the other, 43–42 BC.

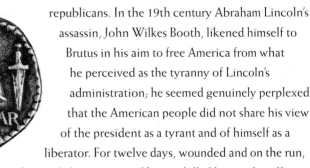

For nearly two thousand years, Caesar's assassination served almost as a model for political murder, beginning to lose its currency only with the rise of anarchism in the 19th century. It provided not only an instantly recognizable scenario – a tyrannical ruler who needs to be removed – but also a moral framework with which to understand, and possibly even applaud, the motives of the assassin, thus providing a justification for an act that would otherwise carry the most severe moral and legal penalties. In the mind of the murderer, if in no one else's, the events of 44 BC even went as far as to ennoble the figure of the assassin. Most crucially, however, they perpetuated the idea that the head of state *is* the state: that the body of the king and the body politic are one and the same. Remove one (according to this theory) and you topple the other. Viewed in this way, assassination became a viable political tactic, guaranteed to bring about a regime change. And yet, time and time again, history would reveal it to be a fallacy.

chapter 2

Turbulent Priest: *Thomas Becket*

By this stroke the sword was dashed upon the pavement and the crown of his head, which was large, was separated from his head in such a way that the blood white with the brain and the brain no less red from the blood, dyed the floor of the cathedral with the white of the lily and the red of the rose, the colours of the Virgin and Mother and of the life and death of the martyr and confessor. The fifth [attacker] ... placed his foot on the neck of the holy priest and precious martyr and, horrible to relate, scattered the brains and blood about the pavement, crying out to the others, 'Let us away, knights, this fellow will rise no more.'[1]

S o reads an eyewitness account of the murder of Thomas Becket, archbishop of Canterbury, at the hands of barons acting on behalf of King Henry II of England. This cold-blooded killing, carried out in 1170, horrified all of Christendom, isolating the English monarch from the rest of Europe and driving a wedge between the English crown and the papacy. Becket's life and death – perhaps the best documented of the time – provide fascinating insights into the politics and personalities of the Middle Ages. Although he was sanctified almost immediately after his death, over 800 years later Thomas Becket has come to be seen by modern historians as an arch villain whose actions caused an irrevocable rift between Rome and the English crown. These two opposing viewpoints illustrate the contradictory nature of a man who started his political career at the right hand of the king and ended it slain by that same king's agents. Even during his lifetime he polarized opinion, fêted in the streets by the common people yet despised by many of his fellow ecclesiastics. As the king's chancellor he was renowned for his love of display and luxury and for his daring on the battlefield, while his piety and devotion to the causes of the church as archbishop of Canterbury contributed to his canonization.

Becket's life and achievements were remarkable by any standards. Born on 21 December, most probably in the year 1118, to a family of Norman merchants in Cheapside, London, he rose from his relatively modest background to gain the highest ecclesiastical position in the land through sheer force of personality and raw talent. Although

The assassination of Thomas Becket was not only a shocking murder, it was an act of the most sacrilegious kind: the killing of an archbishop, the head of the church in England, in his own cathedral. In addition, it was not the last, desperate act of the weak against the strong, but the cynical elimination of an encumbrance by a superior power. It made Becket a martyr. This English alabaster dates to the late 15th century.

contemporary biographies tend to concentrate on the eight eventful years he spent as archbishop, enough details are known about his early life to create a picture of an ambitious, energetic individual. Biographies that appeared in the wake of his canonization (at least eleven were written in the space of twenty years) embellish the bare facts of his early life with omens and portents, revealing the medieval tendency towards hagiography. One later account contributed to the legend of Becket's life by describing his mother as a Saracen princess who had saved Becket's father from death during the Crusades; while pregnant, she had visions of stars and other signs of her child's future significance. As a boy, Becket narrowly escaped death by drowning (a tragically common fate for children at the time) – evidence, according to his biographers, that he was destined for great things.

The facts as they have come down to us are less romantic but no less impressive. As a young man, Thomas of London (as he preferred to be called during his entire lifetime) entered the household of Theobald, then archbishop of Canterbury. Joining this lively and intellectually challenging environment was a crucial step in the ambitious young man's career. Under Theobald's patronage, Thomas was able to study at Europe's leading universities, including Bologna and Auxerre. Although he never undertook his academic work with the seriousness shown by his rival, Gilbert Foliot, who would become bishop of Hereford and later of London, a key account of Becket's life attests to his innate intelligence and his remarkable memory: 'He was so keen in discernment and comprehension that he would always solve difficult questions wisely. His memory was so amazing that whatever he heard of scriptures and legal judgements he was able to cite any time he chose.'[2] Becket may not have begun life with the advantages enjoyed by his contemporaries in Theobald's circle, but his natural abilities saw him through: his studies in Europe allowed him to take up the position of archdeacon at Canterbury, and he became an increasingly trusted member of Theobald's household. Shortly after the coronation of the young Henry II in 1154, Theobald was able to recommend his favourite for the post of chancellor. Thomas Becket now held the highest administrative office in England, second only to the king.

One of Becket's biographers suggests that he was in many ways a skilled actor, able to tailor his personality to whatever the situation demanded.[3] Whether this is evidence of Machiavellian ambition or of a natural tendency for the complexities of the human character to shine in different surroundings, Becket certainly thrived in the company of the new king. Thirty-six years old compared to Henry's twenty-one years,

Reverse of the royal seal of Henry II, showing the energetic and successful king on horseback.

Thomas was the king's most important advisor but soon also became a close companion. In Henry's company the tall, aquiline Thomas – known at Theobald's court as a gentle man prone to stammer – became a vigorous man of action. Henry was impetuous and arrogant, but his youthful energy and generous spirit inspired great loyalty in his men. Lack of judgment and poor advice often led him to make bad political decisions; the king was happiest riding or hunting with falcons, his freckled complexion weatherbeaten no matter the season and his stocky physique kept from corpulence by his incessant movement. He drove his household to distraction, constantly changing plans or deciding to travel on a whim. Thomas, acutely aware that the king's appearance was synonymous with the king's reputation, used the royal coffers to finance ostentatious displays of luxury and wealth intended to show the power of the English crown. When Thomas travelled to France to broker a marriage between Henry's 3-year-old son, also called Henry, and the infant daughter of Louis VII of France, the extravagance of his embassy – which included pack horses ridden by monkeys, 200 members of the chancellor's household and 24 silk outfits for the chancellor himself – dazzled the whole of France. Also at odds with his later incarnation as an ascetic man of the cloth is the fact that Becket took part in the Toulouse military campaign of 1159, taking over the stronghold of Cahors in south-west France along with several other previously impregnable castles and displaying a daring in battle that was remarkable even in an age of warrior-clerics.

When Theobald died in 1161, the position of archbishop of Canterbury fell vacant; after a year, Henry offered it to his chancellor, imagining that the divisions between church and state could be resolved by the close friend who had championed his causes. Becket, rightly concerned that the two roles were incompatible, at first refused. He might have been an obvious choice for the king, but within the ecclesiastical community the worldly, extravagant chancellor would be viewed with suspicion, his loyalties always in doubt. When Becket finally accepted the king's offer, he had to undergo a hasty ordination as a priest before he could become archbishop. His arrival in Canterbury for the investiture ceremony was greeted by ecstatic crowds, while Becket himself, in a foreshadowing of the dramatic conversion to follow, apparently moved among them with humility – according to the contemporary historian Roger of Pontigny, he shed tears as he thought 'less of the honour than the burden'.[4] Gilbert Foliot, soon to emerge as one of Becket's staunchest critics, was unmoved by this show of modesty: 'The king has worked a miracle. Out of a secular man and a soldier he has made an archbishop.'[5]

If the king thought that Becket's appointment would enable him to assert his own interests over those of the church, he was wrong. Within weeks Becket had resigned from his position as chancellor. The easy camaraderie and close affection shared by the king and his chancellor had not translated into their relationship as king and archbishop. Gilbert Foliot wrote that the subsequent rift in relations between church and state was as much a matter of stubborn personalities as ideologies; certainly, there were several occasions during their tempestuous history when even Pope Alexander III, the most sympathetic observer, was frustrated by their obstinacy. Becket saw it much more simply: as archbishop, he was answerable to a greater authority than the king. As holder of the highest ecclesiastical office in the land, he had a duty to defend the needs of the church against the demands of the crown – a reversal of his role as chancellor, in which he had displayed a single-minded rapaciousness in acquiring church funds for the use of the state. After a year of capitulating to the king, Becket began to assert himself, claiming back land and funds that the church had lost under Henry's predecessor, Stephen. At this time Becket underwent a very visible conversion: casting aside the worldly trappings of his previous life, he took part in public displays of humility, every day inviting the poor into his palace where he washed their feet and distributed alms. It is believed that he adopted the hair shirt (discovered under his robes after his death) at around this time.

The first dramatic evidence of discord came early in 1164, over the issue of 'criminous clerks' – the question of whether ecclesiastics convicted of serious offences should be tried by secular or church courts. Since the time of William the Conqueror, the church had been responsible for the sentencing of its own members, which often resulted in lamentably lenient terms for serious crimes. For some time Henry had wanted to deprive clerics of the protection of the church in criminal cases. Becket had initially rejected the king's ideas, which caused Henry to adopt a new strategy, claiming that he was only trying to re-establish rights enjoyed by his predecessors. Under intense pressure, Becket reached a verbal agreement with the king and withdrew his objections. In January 1164 Henry summoned a convocation at Clarendon with the purpose of codifying his reforms and having them formally ratified by Becket and his bishops. But at the final moment Becket dug in his heels once again and refused to append his seal, on the grounds that the king's measures violated canon law. Having reached a stalemate, both parties withdrew, fuming. A relationship that had been based on mutual trust and companionship was now fraught with high drama. Attempts at

Henry II on his throne, arguing with Thomas Becket: an early 14th-century illustration from Peter Langtoft's Chronicle, *a history of England written in Anglo-Norman verse. Becket's conversion from career politician to Christian saint has posed a virtually insoluble problem to modern-day historians.*

reconciliation ended in fierce arguments, and Becket had a gate summarily slammed in his face when he attempted to visit Henry during the course of the summer. In September the king called for another council to be held in Northampton, in order to reassert his authority over his recalcitrant archbishop. In theory, its purpose was to settle a land dispute between one of the king's barons and the church, but in practice it was an attempt to humiliate Becket.

Becket did not help his own cause by failing to appear at the first summons; whether it was a display of his by now notorious obstinacy or whether his chronic ill health had prevented him from attending (he suffered from kidney stones for most of his life), his absence served only to enrage the king. Three weeks later the council convened again, attended by all the bishops of England and Normandy and by the king's barons. The original issue was now almost forgotten (the baron in question was not even in attendance), and in an increasingly rancorous and raucous environment Becket was charged and found guilty of contempt for ignoring the previous summons. His punishment was 'at the king's mercy', which usually involved a fine to be decided by the monarch. But this was only the start of the ordeal: in addition to the charge of contempt, Becket had to answer to accusations of embezzlement during his chancellorship – a charge that was a thinly veiled pretext for the king to exert his control. After days of negotiations and recriminations, during which he was suffering from his chronic health problems, Becket rose from his sick bed for the final day of court. During the proceedings he had compared his tribulations to those of the first Christian martyr, St Stephen. On the morning of the last day of the trial, he made the parallel explicit when he celebrated the Mass of St Stephen, which begins, 'Princes also did sit and speak against me.' In court he eloquently argued his position, that although he was bound in allegiance to the king, his ultimate loyalty was to God. Amid lurid threats from the assembled barons, who gleefully recalled the gruesome fates of previous clerics who had defied their kings, the archbishop's defence was relayed to an apoplectic Henry, who lunged at the company cowering before him. Becket did not stop to wait for the verdict, but fled from the court amid cries of 'traitor' from the king's men.

He left Northampton that night and began to make his way to the coast, travelling under the cover of darkness and eventually setting sail for France from the small port of Eastry in Kent. By leaving the kingdom without the permission of the king – who now referred to his former friend as 'Thomas, formerly archbishop of Canterbury' – Becket only exacerbated his crimes against the crown. He would remain in self-imposed exile in France for six years. The repercussions of his actions were manifold: in abandoning the English clergy, he essentially left them vulnerable to the political might of the monarch. Those who might have supported the archbishop were now left without a leader, and became antagonistic towards the shepherd who had abandoned his flock out of self-preservation. His enemies, on the other hand, saw his flight as proof of his essential perfidy ('The wicked man flees when there is no one pursuing,' claimed the ever hostile Gilbert Foliot[6]). More significantly for Henry, the fact that Becket had decamped to France meant that the rift between king and archbishop was now playing out on an international stage. What had begun in Clarendon as a dispute over specific points of canon law became, at Northampton, a wider argument about historical precedents for state versus church power. By the time of Becket's exile, these specific debates had evolved into more fundamental questions about the extent of the king's authority versus that of God. Becket was clear that his allegiances lay ultimately with God and was received sympathetically by Pope Alexander III, who was himself then in exile

After being humiliated and condemned, Becket flees England for France: a manuscript illumination of about 1310.

at Sens. He also enjoyed the support of the French king Louis VII, causing more diplomatic headaches for the English ruler. Henry's wife, Eleanor of Aquitaine, had at one time been married to Louis; and with her marriage to Henry his domains in France had been significantly extended. Relations between the two monarchs were thus already complicated without the added controversy of Becket's exile. The pope's involvement was even more of a diplomatic minefield: one of the purposes of the Constitutions of Clarendon had been to curtail the papacy's involvement in English affairs, so the pontiff was obliged to negotiate a perilous path between backing the archbishop and not antagonizing the English king.

The view from France was that Becket had won the moral victory, and with Pope Alexander's support and considerable diplomacy he should have been able to bring Henry round to an agreement. But the archbishop himself seemed to become only more self-righteous and inflexible. Even his clerk, John of Salisbury – one of Becket's greatest supporters and a moderate and gentle man – sadly noted the archbishop's zealousness and lack of tact, writing that 'from the first, with mistaken zeal, he provoked the king … to bitterness, whereas some consideration should have been given to time, to place, and to persons'.[7] By now the possibility of compromise had long since passed, and Becket believed that the only way to make Henry see reason was to threaten him with excommunication – the most powerful weapon in the ecclesiastic arsenal. Accompanying Becket's confidence in his spiritual authority was an intensified programme of reflection and penitence. It was while staying at the Cistercian abbey of Pontigny in Burgundy that he had adopted a frugal monastic life, wearing the monk's habit, sleeping little, if at all, on a rough wooden pallet, and eating sparingly. Even the monks marvelled at his enthusiasm for physical mortification – he would immerse himself in cold streams and scourge himself frequently, and wore the hair shirt as part of his spiritual diet. The transformation from worldly chancellor to ascetic man of the cloth could not have been more complete, and served to emphasize the extent of the gulf between the archbishop and the king.

After two years of monastic life Becket undertook a pilgrimage to the Cluniac abbey of Vézelay, where two years earlier some new relics had been discovered, adding to its already impressive collection. Among them were fragments of clothing believed to have been worn by Shadrach, Meshach and Abednego; these were of particular interest to Becket, who saw parallels between his own situation and the three who had been punished for not worshipping an image of the king of Babylon. All signs seemed to point to the church as the location for the next move against Henry. Invited by the abbot of Vézelay to celebrate High Mass on Whitsunday, 12 June 1166, Becket followed up his elegant and well-received sermon with a deed that astounded his listeners: after describing the standoff between himself and the king, he swiftly denounced and excommunicated eight of his enemies, among them leading clerics of England. He concluded with a threat of excommunication to Henry if he did not repent, and wrote him several letters to that effect. The king, however, remained unmoved. Becket's liberal use of the power of excommunication had raised the stakes, undermining the king's authority categorically and forcibly involving more people in the conflict. Henry retaliated by gathering the might of the English bishops around him, and asserted his power through every means possible. Becket's remaining years of exile were punctuated by attempts by the pope to negotiate a reconciliation between the two, but the archbishop grew to despair that such a stage would ever be reached, claiming that only his death would terminate the conflict. Finally, after Henry and Becket had sent several envoys to argue their respective cases before the pope, but to

Two scenes from the Becket Leaves, *the eight remaining pages of a 13th-century manuscript describing the life of Becket. In the first, Becket pronounces his sentence of excommunication while his listeners shrink in horror; and in the second, Becket argues his case before Henry II of England and Louis VII of France.*

no avail, the apparent impasse was resolved by the king's decision to hold a coronation for his eldest son.

In order to ensure his line of succession, Henry II had wanted the young Prince Henry to be crowned during his lifetime. To preside at the coronation was a privilege normally reserved for the archbishop of Canterbury, but that was clearly impossible in this case. In a devastating affront to ecclesiastical protocol and a personal blow to Becket, Prince Henry was crowned in Westminster Abbey on 14 June 1170 by Roger, archbishop of York, assisted by Gilbert Foliot (as bishop of London) and the bishop of Salisbury, among others. This was apparently the catalyst needed to reach an agreement, and ten days after the coronation Henry II arrived in France to meet the papal commissioners. He agreed to all the terms laid out yet refused to bestow the symbolic kiss of peace, which would have been unequivocal proof of his forgiveness. The news was relayed to Becket, who was still not entirely convinced and was reluctant to meet the king without a formal invitation. The two finally met at Fréteval, midway between Chartres and Tours; after six years of obstinacy on both sides, the king agreed, quite simply and with little fanfare, to everything the archbishop demanded. Becket himself later described in a letter to the pope how the king spoke 'with such intimacy that it seemed as if there had never been any discord between us'.[8] It is possible that Henry, worried that his recently crowned 15-year-old son, left alone in England, would fall under the sway of conniving courtiers, wanted back his old advisor and confidant. Becket had no shortage of adversaries in England, who would provide a check to any potential cabals at court. It was agreed that Becket should return to England.

But relations between the two were not fully restored, and the diplomatic wrangling continued. Becket had insisted on a visible manifestation of the king's blessing on his return to England: if the kiss of peace was not going to be offered, he expected a royal escort by way of public expression of welcome. In fact, the escort he received when he finally landed in Kent on 1 December 1170 was, if anything, a harbinger of the difficulties Becket would face now he was back in England. He was met only by John of Oxford, one of the bishops he had excommunicated at Vézelay and with whom, not surprisingly, he shared a relationship of mutual antipathy. To further complicate matters, before leaving France Becket had sent letters suspending the key figures who had taken part in the young Henry's coronation – the archbishop of York and the attendant bishops – and had renewed the excommunication of the bishop of Salisbury and of Gilbert Foliot. There were many powerful men back in England who had plenty to

e dult mall dvir h̄le med̄e　　　　Ouant en engleterre ariue　　　　lur̄ q̄ uvt i parueniftes
e flur̄ meut q̄t uaut atend̄　　　coure latendent ala riue　　　les euesques lu roi meister
k e deftre hastufe e engvs　　　Pouret h̄ ſa beneicū　　　　n ſentence eſcumāciū
P ar quei repentron apres　　D emandent par deuociū　　D urt ſurſe eſt la cōtentiū
L arceues q̄ lur reſpūt　　　cō auf reaut demad̄ puī quei　　S lui urt dir a grāt manace
H e place adeu ki ſuſ le mūd　S uſpent les plaz lu rei　　S i noſtre ſurs le roi ſace
k e io pur tāut tel pour ete　　　C ele part ſunt alez toſt　　rez ett murt e eſmeu
k e de mū i̇ſp̄t me retreie　　　Ouant la nef eſtoit ueūe　　　e ne li ſera paſ teu
e ngleterre uoi io de ti　　　P ar la croiz ſu toſt eſmue　　H e ſlarta kil ne ſe māenge
o i enterai ſi ſai de ſi　　　L i paiſant tou iole en uiit　　e gref uengāce de ro pronge
A tur ne meſt occiſiū　　　k e tut iacurrū ſuit　　　k eſtoſt auez medle
D e mort iſuſtrai paſſiū　　　C uf eſturcez e trebabat　　T ur le regne e le clerge
ſiſt lau del incarnatiū　　　C n la mer cunt lur plat　　arceueſq̄ lur ir e rage
Cum nuſē eſcrit liſū　　　V unt p̄ li receiure a tote　　P ar ſen e ſimpletce aſſuage
cō il e cent ſeiſſante e diſ　　D iere li uī hauʒ kiſ lote　　e lur dulc ſeignurs ſacez
D e ſun exil ſerme meſt uit　　B enoit ſeir bi eſt ueneiz　　H en ſera paſ ti droit ueʒ
e l ſecund iur v terz daduent　　C l nun deu ſoir recreir　　H e ſui paſ en ceſte aſaire
S e mit en mer puceinent　　　taut eſū ueneſt buiant　　A u roi nan regne auenture
P ar nuit ſariua a ſandwiz　　Cheualſ arme e ſergant　　A ſa bone uoillance e gu
e ſort do douere uuit eſchunt　　D e ſaluer le en uūt deſpir　　D oirz eſt ke iuſtice fait
P ur les aguvtz deſ armez　　A grant ȝorȝeet li uit dir　　e ceuſ ſunt ſair ſor enple
k a douere ſunt deuutiez　　P ur quei auez par coȝgil　　D euſt mort e ma igliſe ſal cōm enpere
Quant lunt oi cil a grit oſt　　La tre uiſe en tel triboil　　D e me ſuȝeʒ nomecmer la ſu uetr

The archbishop arrived back in Kent in December 1170. This illustration from the Becket Leaves shows supporters coming out to greet him in a little boat while a crowd waits on shore – including two soldiers who warn him not to land.

This illustration, dating to around 1180, is the earliest known depiction of Becket's martyrdom. The top section shows the four knights arriving as Becket is dining, while the bottom half shows his murder (left) and the knights doing penance at his shrine (right).

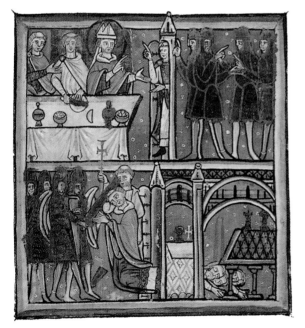

lose with Becket's return; his parting letters from France were the final nail in his coffin.

Upon his arrival, Becket took a circuitous route back to Canterbury, on the one hand to allow his supporters to celebrate his return, and on the other to allow him to evade agents of the king who were dismayed at his letters of excommunication. Ecstatic crowds met the archbishop along the route to Canterbury. Once within the town walls, he made his way barefoot to the cathedral amid great public rejoicing. The official response, however, was somewhat chillier. The king's agents soon apprehended the archbishop and demanded that he absolve the excommunicates. He refused, after which relations with the crown began to worsen. The de Broc family, meanwhile, who were comfortably ensconced in the former archiepiscopal castle of Saltwood, were fearful of what they stood to lose now that Becket had returned. Various offences against Becket were carried out at their command, ranging from the seizure of his goods and the arrest of his men to farcical insults such as the docking of his horse's tail. The situation was highly volatile.

Henry II was celebrating Christmas at the castle of Bur-le-Roi, near Bayeux in Normandy, when he learnt of the troubles surrounding Becket in England. That the king was rash and prone to outbursts is well documented. After years of diplomatic negotiations and endless argument, it appeared that his reconciliation with Becket had been a failure. Exasperated, he lashed out, tearing his clothes in frustration – 'What disloyal cowards do I have in my court; will no one rid me of this turbulent priest?'[9] – and effectively signed Becket's death warrant.

There is no true consensus as to why the king uttered these words; some believe that the frustrated king was not issuing an order for Becket's execution but merely speaking metaphorically, while one account relates a conversation in which the king is advised to settle matters by hanging his archbishop at the end of a rope.[10] Henry later denied issuing any direct order, and was overwhelmed by remorse once he heard how events had unfolded. Nevertheless, four of his barons – Reginald FitzUrse, William de Tracey, Hugh de Moreville and Richard le Breton – had taken the king at his word. That evening, they stole away from the castle and left France by different ports, their ships 'guided by the devil'.[11] (It is worth noting how their secretive behaviour was not compatible with the correct execution of an official warrant.) Arriving in England, they made their way to Saltwood Castle, where under the guidance of Ranulf de Broc they summoned local garrison forces and planned their attack.

There are five contemporary accounts of the death of Thomas Becket. All were set down within twenty years of his death, and were written either by his clerks, who knew him very well (John of Salisbury, William Fitzstephen and Herbert of Bosham), or by those who were close enough to count as reputable sources (Edward Grim and Benedict of Peterborough). Of these, only Edward Grim actually witnessed Becket's murder; he tried to protect him, and is often depicted in stained glass or other artworks attempting to shield the archbishop from the onslaught. Each account varies in detail to some extent, but in the main they agree on the sequence of events. On the morning of 29 December 1170 the knights set out for Canterbury, about 15 miles (24 km) away. Once they had reached the cathedral complex, Ranulf took the gatehouse while the four barons, accompanied by other knights, made their way to archbishop's palace and demanded to see Becket, who had retired to his chamber after dining. Threatening and clamorous, they confronted him, insisting once again that he revoke the excommunications, claiming that they were evidence of his lack of support for the king's newly crowned son. Becket, cold and unmoved, stated his devotion to the young king but refused to absolve the prelates, which was in any event an issue for the pope. As the knights grew more aggressive, Becket's monks, recognizing the danger he was in, begged him to seek sanctuary in the cathedral. He was reluctant to do so, and had to be forcibly dragged from his antechamber to the church doors. Once inside, the frantic monks, hearing the clatter of the approaching knights who were now fully armed, attempted to bar the door. Becket refused: 'It is not right to turn the house of prayer … into a fortress.'[12]

By mid-afternoon in the depths of winter, the cathedral would have been in gloomy twilight, with the sound of the monks singing vespers resounding around its stone walls. As Becket approached the altar of the Virgin Mary in the north transept – by now almost completely alone, having been abandoned by his clerks – he was accosted by the four knights, who accused him of treason and once again demanded absolution for the excommunicated clerics. When Becket refused, they threatened to kill him. One of the most significant accounts of the assassination is that of Edward Grim, a visitor who was with the archbishop at the time of the attack and who was severely wounded in the arm as he attempted

A 15th-century illustration of the murder. The four knights strike Becket while he kneels before the altar of the Virgin Mary. There are five contempory accounts of Becket's death, but only one – that of Edward Grim – was provided by an eyewitness. Grim describes Becket saying, 'I am prepared to die for my Lord.'

to protect him from their blows. He describes a stoical Becket reacting with calm dignity to the knights' barbarous behaviour. 'I am prepared to die for my Lord', he said, 'so that in my blood the church may find liberty and peace.'[13] Grim's account portrays Becket as a martyr, calling him a 'sacrificial lamb' in contrast to the sacrilegious knights who carried weapons in a holy place. It continues to relate how Becket offered himself up to the sword 'as a living sacrifice', remaining unmovable as the knights began to strike. At the third blow, Becket fell to his knees, saying, 'For the name of Jesus and the wellbeing of the church I am prepared to embrace death.' As he lay face downwards, he received a fourth and fatal blow. The final desecration was carried out by a fifth man, Hugh of Horsea, a cleric of Ranulf de Broc aptly known as Mauclerc. To the horror of the assembling onlookers, he placed his foot on the neck of the fallen man and scattered his brains across the cathedral floor. Assured of Becket's death, the assailants left the cathedral, leaving the prostrate body of the archbishop to be mourned by his monks.

The barons looted and ransacked the archbishop's palace, attacking its servants and stealing its horses. The horrified monks, afraid that Becket's body would be dragged from the cathedral and desecrated, hastened to bury it. In doing so, they discovered that, beneath his costly robes, Becket had worn a monk's habit and a verminous hair shirt that stretched from his neck to his knees. Such evidence of the man's private piety would contribute to the myth that grew up around him.

Becket's death affected Henry II greatly. Upon hearing the news, he was visibly distraught and went into seclusion for three days, mourning the death of his former friend. Politically, his reputation was in tatters, and his subsequent invasion of Ireland can be seen as an attempt to reassert political power by bringing that country back under the control of Rome. As penance for his part in Becket's murder, in May 1172 Henry was obliged by the pope's legates at Avranches to concede all points of the Constitutions of Clarendon, granting Becket in death what had eluded him in his lifetime. In addition, he was expected to fund two hundred knights, at a cost of £9,000 each, to fight in the Crusades. In 1174, once Becket had been elevated to sainthood, Henry performed a elaborate display of spiritual remorse at his shrine: after approaching the cathedral on foot, divested of his kingly robes, Henry was publicly flogged – receiving six strokes from each of the six bishops, and three strokes each from eighty of the cathedral's monks. He then spent the night in prayer, prostrate at the shrine.

Many contemporary accounts of Becket's life were written within a few years of the assassination, after his cult had spread like wildfire throughout Europe. Descriptions such as that written by Edward Grim suggesting Becket was aware of his impending death and was prepared to martyr himself for his cause are part of a wider trend in which medieval chroniclers compared Thomas Becket to Christ. Many of his biographers emphasized the timing of the event, noting how Becket's arrival back in England coincided with the beginning of Advent. Becket's return to Canterbury was compared to Christ's arrival into Jerusalem; he was disturbed following dinner, which paralleled the

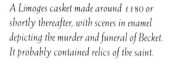

A Limoges casket made around 1180 or shortly thereafter, with scenes in enamel depicting the murder and funeral of Becket. It probably contained relics of the saint.

Becket's shrine became one of the most popular pilgrimage centres in the whole of Europe, bringing large sums of money to Canterbury. Badges like these were acquired in large numbers to prove that the wearer had completed his or her journey.

Last Supper; his replies to the knights drew directly from or alluded to scripture; and the five blows were compared with the five wounds of Christ.

The cult of Thomas Becket had begun almost immediately after his death. As news of the murder spread, the people of Canterbury gathered at the place he had fallen, dipping torn fragments of clothing into the still-fresh blood on the floor. Within twenty-four hours the first miracle was reported: a local woman was cured of paralysis after bathing in water with which this blood had been mixed. Later, tiny amounts of the remaining blood would be scraped from the stone floor and mixed with water in small vials to be sold as the 'water of St Thomas', an extremely popular miracle cure for all manner of ailments. By Easter 1171, when the cathedral was reopened, the cult had become firmly established, and pilgrims flocked from all over Europe to pay homage to the martyr, whose miracles had now spread beyond the immediate vicinity of Canterbury to the whole of England and would soon arrive in Continental Europe. On Ash Wednesday 1173 – little more than two years after the archbishop's death – Pope Alexander canonized Thomas Becket. Canterbury developed into one of the most important pilgrimage sites of Europe, and images depicting his martyrdom and miracles were frequent themes in medieval iconography, such as the series of stained-glass 'Miracle Windows' in Canterbury Cathedral itself. Pilgrims were a great source of income, and many of the more exalted visitors made substantial contributions to the coffers of the diocese. King Louis VII donated a ruby the size of an apricot, known as the 'Régale de France'; it was the largest ever known. This jewel was incorporated into the costly and elaborate shrine created in 1220 to provide a focus of veneration. Raised on steps, the casket holding Becket's remains was decorated with gold trelliswork and encrusted with pearls and gems. 'The least valuable portion was of gold, but every part glistened, shone, sparkled with rare and very large jewels, some of them larger than a

opposite *The Corona – a circular chapel at the extreme east end of Canterbury Cathedral – was built in 1182–84 to house the relic of St Thomas's scalp. The work would have been paid for by the donations of many pilgrims.*

goose's egg,' wrote a dazzled Erasmus in 1513.[14] The shrine lasted until 1538, when it was broken up by Henry VIII. Although the veneration of Becket continued in Catholic Europe, he was desanctified in the Church of England, dismissed by Henry as a traitor to the crown: 'from hense forth the sayde Thomas Becket shall not be esteemed, named, reputed, nor called a sayncte, but bysshop Becket.'[15] The 'Régale de France' was made into a thumb ring.

During Becket's lifetime, the philosophical argument for the justification of assassination had been re-evaluated by his own clerk, John of Salisbury, who in 1159 had written his *Policraticus* on the subject of tyrannicide. This was, however, a continuation of the old debate begun in antiquity about the morality of removing a capricious or unjust ruler from power; although it would become a point of reference over the coming centuries, it was an academic treatise rather than an assassin's charter. Becket's assassination could not, and did not, form part of that philosophical debate, but it was shocking in the extreme, both in its literal and metaphorical senses. In our secular age, we may find it hard to appreciate the significance of a murder in a sanctuary, but to Becket's contemporaries it was an act of unspeakable horror. The church provided the ultimate haven – a place of guaranteed safety and protection from any worldly authority, no matter how high. That the life of the king's own archbishop could not be safeguarded within its walls was inconceivable, and represented the ultimate act of transgression by the crown. The murder of the archbishop by the king's own men said more

In this manuscript of about 1520, the poet John Lydgate – a contemporary of Geoffrey Chaucer, and himself influenced by the Canterbury Tales *– is shown leaving Canterbury with a group of pilgrims.*

about the power struggles between church and state than any number of excommunications ever could.

Whatever Henry's precise intentions regarding Becket, he had failed utterly to rid himself of his troublesome enemy. Becket had now transcended the highest ecclesiastical position in the land to become the most popular saint in England, and would be venerated throughout Europe for hundreds of years. But Becket was no ordinary saint. Most Christian martyrs achieved sainthood through their refusal to repudiate Christ; Becket's 'martyrdom' was the result of questions of principle. Having refused to capitulate to the demands of the king, he was venerated for his integrity.[16] In the popular imagination, Becket's stance was the ultimate act of defiance against tyrannical rule, upholding the law of God over the law of the monarch at all costs. Veneration of St Thomas Becket became in itself a political act, a way of expressing hostility to the monarch without fear of reprisal. The archbishop's reputation was re-evaluated in the late 20th century, when his alleged integrity was dismissed as mere gesture politics and his actions condemned for the divisive effect they had on England.[17] As for Henry, his part in the murder alienated him from most of Europe and was a contributing factor in the Barons' Revolt of 1173, the year that Becket was made a saint.

opposite *Pope John Paul II and the archbishop of Canterbury, Robert Runcie, kneel together at the spot where Becket was slain, 28 May 1982.*

chapter 3

To Kill a King: *Henri IV*

The streets of Paris in the early 17th century were nothing like the wide, tree-lined boulevards for which the city is known today. Narrow passages and gloomy *allées* crisscrossed the urban fabric, making it quicker to travel on foot than in the ostentatious coaches favoured by the nobility. Designed for an altogether more spacious environment, these cumbersome vehicles, drawn by up to six horses, overwhelmed the city's streets, forcing pedestrians up against the walls of the surrounding buildings as they rumbled past.

The Rue de la Ferronnerie, in the area of Paris now known as Les Halles, was a notoriously congested street. It bordered the Cimetière des Innocents, which, despite its insalubrious air and almost palpable stench, was a curiously popular meeting place for both commercial transactions and romantic liaisons. At times it seemed as if all of Paris's social strata converged on this spot: hawkers, noblemen, soldiers, thieves, and everywhere merchants and tradesmen of all kinds, with ware-laden carts blocking the streets and bringing traffic to a standstill. Paris at this time was the largest city in Europe, with a population nearing 400,000. All walks of life jostled together in cramped accommodation, and it was common to live and work in the same building. One of the largest social groups was made up of casual labourers; these were usually young men from the provinces, attracted to the city in the age-old quest for fortune. They roamed the alleys, seeking whatever opportunities might arise, legitimate or otherwise. Street crime – particularly violent street crime – was rife.

King Henri IV had already undertaken a series of successful building projects throughout the city. Among his ambitious schemes were the completion of the Pont Neuf (now one of the oldest bridges in Paris), the Place Dauphine at the western tip of the Île de la Cité, and the serenely beautiful square now known as the Place des Vosges. Improving the flow of traffic around Rue de la Ferronnerie was just one of his many plans for urban development.

On the afternoon of 14 May 1610, Henri IV was travelling in his carriage from the Tuileries, heading east to the Arsenal to call on his finance minister, the duc de Sully, who was ill in bed and unable to join

The arrest of Henri IV's assassin, in a dramatic painting by Charles-Gustave Housez (1860). The narrow streets are an accurate reflection of much of 17th-century Paris, whose confined spaces would have enabled François Ravaillac to approach the king with relative ease.

the king at court. Henri was accompanied by three courtiers, among them the duc d'Épernon, favourite of the previous king, Henri III, and now colonel-general of the infantry. Progress was slow, but the day was fine; and although the behemoth of a carriage lurched through the traffic, at times almost grazing the walls of the buildings lining the streets, its awnings were down, allowing the passengers to enjoy the decorations that had been prepared in honour of the queen's arrival in Paris the next day. Henri had come out without his glasses, and asked Épernon to read him a letter during the journey. The duke did so, sitting companionably close to the king, one arm draped around his shoulders.

The coach juddered to a halt and, since there was no sign of the traffic being about to move off, a footman jumped down and ran ahead to see what was causing the delay. At that moment, a tall figure with flaming red hair leapt from the crowd and onto the coach, seeming to fill the open window. In the confusion the king was left defenceless. He was stabbed three times, the knife severing his aorta and puncturing a lung. The duc d'Épernon covered the now unconscious king with a cloak, hiding the blood pouring from his mouth from the horrified crowd and attempting to soothe their distress by claiming that the wound was not serious. Henri was hurried to the Louvre, while messengers ran on foot to alert the court's physicians. Whether their medical expertise would have been sufficient to keep the king alive was immaterial. France's beloved king – 'le bon Henri', 'le vert galant' – was dead on arrival.

The king's assassin – François Ravaillac, a fanatical Catholic – had not tried to escape. After the fatal blows, he dropped back from the carriage and allowed the surrounding crowd to seize him without offering any resistance. It was as though, having achieved his aim, he was ready to relinquish his own life. 'I have done what I came to do,' he would later claim under interrogation.

'Le roi est mort!' With the king's death, Paris entered a period of almost frenzied mourning. As the diarist Pierre de Lestoile recorded at the time, 'Shops were shut, everyone, young and old, was caught up in an orgy of weeping and wailing. Some of the women and girls actually tore their hair.'[1] But this went beyond mere sentiment. France had not only lost a popular king, it was thrown into political crisis. The heir to the throne, Louis XIII, was only eight years old, and his mother the queen, the Italian Marie de' Medici, now became regent. Her lack of experience was not the only concern: crucially, she was foreign, and, for a country only recently enjoying a period of peace after decades of religious warfare, this was potentially calamitous. Personally, too, she had her detractors. At court she was known to be quarrelsome

Frans Pourbus the Younger, King Henri IV of France, c. *1610.*
This portrait was painted not long before the king's death.

and to harbour petty jealousies, and she was widely believed to be intellectually inferior to Henri, who had been recognized for his quick intelligence and lively wit.

Yet, for all Henri's popularity, this was by no means the first attempt on his life. Historians differ, but it seems that Henri had been the target of some sixteen to twenty attacks during his reign. Nearly a decade before his fatal encounter with Ravaillac, Henri had written in a letter, 'Every day I discover the greatest evil-doings, perfidies, ingratitudes and plots against me which you could ever believe.'[2] Earlier still, he had complained that his people were 'so lacking in gratitude toward their king ... as to make constant demands upon his life'.[3] Why, when he had done so much for France's stability, was he the target of so many assassination attempts?

Henri's ascent to the throne had been controversial from the outset. His predecessor, Henri III, was an indolent, dissolute figure, renowned for his coterie of dandies – 'les Mignons' – and for his scandalous pleasure-seeking. He had been assassinated by a fanatical Dominican, Jacques Clément, in 1589, and the Bourbon Henri de Navarre was put forward as his rightful successor. Critics remarked that his claim to the throne was tenuous – Henri de Navarre was related to the king only in the 'twenty-second degree' – but most alarming for Catholic France was the fact that he had been raised a Huguenot.

The religion of the king of France was of profound importance to the state. The king was not only called upon to uphold the Catholic

faith, but in many ways he was its embodiment – a belief expressed succinctly in the traditional saying 'Une foi, une loi, un roi' ('One faith, one law, one king'). The coronation ceremony, established in the 9th century and traditionally held in Reims Cathedral, was a potent symbol of this inextricable connection between crown and church. During the coronation the French king was proclaimed 'Sa Majesté Très Chrètienne' ('His Most Christian Majesty') and anointed with holy oil. The oath he made to his subjects included a promise to protect the country from heretics; since 1540 and the advent of the Reformed church in France, this would have been understood to include the Protestant Huguenots. Upon completion of the ceremony, the king was thought to be invested with divine powers (the 13th-century king Louis IX had even been canonized), as illustrated by the traditional belief that he was able to cure scrofula – popularly known as the 'king's evil' – simply by touch. Since the French had already suffered decades of religious warfare, the faith of their future king – whether, as one historian expressed it, he prayed in the Latin of the Catholic church or the French of the Reformed church – was of great consequence.

Henri's faith had been of political significance since his birth, in December 1553. His betrothal at the age of three to Marguerite de Valois, sister of the then king Charles IX, had been an attempt to reconcile the French crown and the Huguenot faith. That aim ended in bloody tragedy years later, when their marriage in Paris in August 1572 formed the background to the episode of murderous violence against

Huguenots known as the St Bartholomew's Day Massacre. Historians still debate whether the full extent of the massacre had been orchestrated at government level or whether it had been a spontaneous demonstration of religious hatred that had been coming for many years. On the eve of the wedding, there were signs that the barely suppressed fear and resentment of the Huguenot religion was about to erupt. In the streets and taverns, rumours abounded about the strange practices of these heretical people: it was said that they kidnapped and slaughtered Catholic children, that they committed blasphemy and profaned the Host. Fanatical sermons boomed from the pulpits of Paris, urging people to execute the heretics in order to secure their own salvation. 'God will not suffer this execrable coupling,' warned the curé of Saint-Paul in the Marais about the impending marriage. As large numbers of Huguenot wedding guests assembled in the crowded city, which was simmering in the heat of late

Three days of bloody violence – known as the St Bartholomew's Day Massacre – followed Henri's marriage to his first wife, Marguerite de Valois, in August 1572. The Huguenot victims numbered in their thousands. The massacre was sparked off by the murder of the Protestant Admiral de Coligny in the early hours of 24 August. A print by Frans Hogenberg (above) shows the admiral being attacked in his bedchamber and then thrown out of the window, while Joseph-Benoît Suvée's painting (1787; opposite) attempts a more heroic reconstruction.

summer, tensions continued to rise. These austere, dark-clad noblemen seemed to fill the streets, filling onlookers with a sense of foreboding.

The St Bartholomew's Day Massacre was one of a long series of attacks against French Huguenots. On this occasion, the violence was precipitated by the murder of Admiral Gaspard de Coligny – one of the Huguenots' political leaders – at the order of the Catholic duc de Guise, who was head of one of France's most powerful families. In the early hours of 24 August, six days after Henri's marriage to Marguerite de Valois, members of the king's guard, accompanied by the duke and other nobles, broke into Coligny's house, ran him through with a sword and threw his lifeless body out the window. His severed head was taken to the Louvre as proof of the deed (it was later embalmed and sent to the pope as a trophy), while his body was dragged through the streets by a Catholic mob – an act of desecration commonly meted out to criminals – and three days later hung from a gibbet. It is uncertain whether the duc de Guise was acting on orders from Charles IX to rid Paris of Huguenots, whether Catherine de' Medici had a role to play in provoking the slaughter, or whether it just took the merest whisper of rumour to spark off violence, but within a matter of days the river Seine was flowing red with the blood of butchered Protestants.

An estimated 1,000 people – some historians suspect the number to have been twice that – were killed in a frenzy of bloodlust. By the end of the month the mob's fury seemed to have burnt itself out, only to spread to the provinces, where the massacres continued well into the autumn.

The Catholic reaction was one of crowing celebration. A popular rumour at the time, that a barren hawthorn bush in the Cimetière des Innocents had sprung into flower, was interpreted as a sign that God approved of this purging of infidels. The Vatican had long urged France to adopt more radical measures against the growing Huguenot population, and in Rome a celebratory Te Deum was held, as well as a triumphant ceremony in the French church of San Luigi dei Francesi.

A medal produced in Rome in 1572 to commemorate the St Bartholomew's Day Massacre. On one side is a portrait of Pope Gregory XIII, while on the reverse a vengeful angel oversees a mound of murdered Huguenots.

To confirm the pope's official sanction of the massacre, a commemorative medal was struck, with the profile of the pontiff on one side and an angel overseeing the slaughter on the other. Another, similar medallion showed King Charles IX standing triumphant over a pile of Huguenot limbs and disembodied heads. Within the Vatican itself, a series of frescoes commemorating the event were commissioned from the painter Giorgio Vasari.

The French clergy, urged on by Rome, welcomed back into the Catholic faith those Huguenots who remained in France, on the condition that they renounce Protestantism in writing and accept the full legal implications of their heresy. An estimated 5,000 Huguenots converted to, or returned to, Catholicism, and the church coffers swelled with donations from former Protestants. At court, Henri's choice was stark: he could convert to Catholicism, spend the rest of his life in the Bastille, or face execution. In the event, he chose to change his faith – neither the first nor the last time he would do so. He wrote to the pope to ask forgiveness on 3 October 1572, swearing to renounce Protestantism. Now Henri was essentially a prisoner at court, forced to live among the de Guise family as though the massacre had never taken place.

Four years later, in 1576, Henri was able to flee to the provinces, where he rallied Protestant forces. Now that his life no longer depended on it, he lost no time in abjuring his Catholic faith, and on 5 February of that year declared his Protestantism in the cathedral of Tours. The powerful Catholic League, headed by the duc de Guise and supported by the pope and Philip II of Spain, refused to accept that he was the rightful heir and attacked him both politically and personally. His

*Paris during the time of Henri IV,
from Braun and Hogenberg's* Civitates
Orbis Terrarum, *1573–1618.*

character was corrupt, claimed the League, citing as proof his hypocrisy and his vacillation between faiths when political expediency required it. Satirical texts circulated, attempting to undermine his authority. He was depicted as a fool and a lecher, ruled only by his appetites, or accused of acts of desecration against the Catholic church. Henri was forced to the south of France, from where he undertook a long series of wars against the League, attempting to take over the country province by province.

Finally, in 1589, even as Henri continued to fight against the Catholic League, King Henri III was assassinated and the Protestant Henri ascended to the French throne. He was a brilliant military strategist who inspired loyalty in his troops, but he realized that in order to win the hearts of his people and to gain the upper hand – particularly in the nation's capital, which would never accept a Protestant king – he would need to convert once more to Catholicism. 'Paris', Henri is reported to have said (probably apocryphally, but the comment is certainly in his quick-witted style) 'is certainly worth a mass.' Thus Henri renounced Protestantism for the final time in 1593 and entered the city; his coronation ceremony took place in Chartres Cathedral the following year. In reverting to Catholicism, he helped unite his country but also ensured that he would be a constant target for religious extremists. Some would always see him as a heretic whose conversion had been just for show. As one of his subjects was reported to lament, 'The king is now lost: from this moment he is killable.'[4]

When Henri announced his intentions to convert, in the summer of 1593, he had not yet received absolution from the pope. This left him in a vulnerable position, since he could still be perceived as a heretic by the more fanatical adherents to the Catholic faith. It was during this period that one of the many attempts on his life was made. Pierre Barrière, a boatman from Orléans, had sought an audience with the king in order to get close enough to stab him. Such a method, which offered no escape route, indicates that the king's potential assassins were prepared to martyr themselves – as would become evident during Ravaillac's testimony. Barrière was apprehended before he could cause any harm, but the incident drew attention to the Jesuits, who were suspected of being behind the attempt. At the time the Jesuits were widely thought to advocate tyrannicide; although they merely continued the old philosophical debate about the nature of tyranny, they were widely mistrusted and were believed to be behind many plots and conspiracies. The order's connection with the subject of tyrannicide would become more firmly established with the appearance of the *De rege et regis institutione* ('On the King and the Institution of Kingship'), written by the Spanish Jesuit Juan de Mariana in 1599, which argued that it was lawful to depose a tyrannical ruler. The idea that Henri was a tyrant *in titula* – that his former Protestantism had excluded him from a legitimate claim to the throne, and that he had therefore come to it by unlawful means – was a motivation for many of the attempts on his life, providing a justification for his would-be assassins. One of the most serious attempts was by a young law student, Jacques Chastel (sometimes spelled Châtel), who succeeded in stabbing the king, although the attack caused only minor injuries to his face. Chastel was executed and the Jesuits were once more implicated in the plot – incorrectly – and temporarily expelled from the kingdom. However, their alleged views had lodged in the popular consciousness: the question of how far Ravaillac had been influenced by Jesuit doctrine would form part of his interrogation.

François Ravaillac was by all accounts a pitiful figure. During his gruelling interrogation, the facts of his life were revealed in great detail, which have been used many times to shed light on his motives for killing the monarch. He was born in 1578 near Angoulême, some 300 miles (480 km) from Paris ('seven days' walk', he would explain), and had grown up in poverty, one of six children whose father had abandoned their mother. As adults, most of the family remained estranged from Ravaillac and from his elderly mother, who without his help would have been reduced to begging in the street. His father and brother, who lived locally, had been involved in public disputes and accused of theft, blackening the family name and reducing Ravaillac's chances of acquiring a respectable trade. He scraped a living in the lowest ranks of the judiciary at Angoulême, working as a scribe, and then became a valet. In the two years before Henri's assassination he supplemented this work by teaching reading, writing and the catechism to local children. Catholicism played an important part in Ravaillac's life

François Ravaillac, the assassin of Henri IV, brandishes the murder weapon. A Catholic with extremist views, he had become convinced that Henri was about to wage war on the pope. Engraving by Christoffel van Sichem the Elder, c. 1610–20.

and that of his contemporaries. Angoulême at that time has been described as 'an island of ultra-Catholic League supporters in a sea of Huguenots'.[5] At his trial, Ravaillac described the king as a heretic and returned repeatedly to his belief that 'the king had wanted to make war on the pope'[6] as a reason for the murder. It seemed that Ravaillac's religious fervour went beyond that of the usual practising Catholic, and it even emerged that he experienced apocalyptic visions.

As a young man Ravaillac had attempted to join the Feuillants, a branch of the Cistercian order renowned for its extreme asceticism. Vows of silence and mortification of the flesh were central to its observances. Monks knelt on the floor to eat meagre dishes of oats and barley, and slept on bare planks of wood. Self-flagellation was common; coupled with extreme fasting, it had contributed to the deaths of several monks. Despite these hardships, the order swelled in size with the admission of eager postulants like Ravaillac. His time within the community was to be brief, however: whether or not his already fragile state of mind had been further affected by the extreme privations of the order, he soon fell prey to visions. Sounds of trumpets – the clarion call of heaven – were accompanied by the smell of sulphur, which he interpreted as a symbol of the purgatory that would be suffered by heretical Protestants. He saw a group of armed men, which he believed to be a premonition of war against the pope. The Feuillants, who disapproved of mysticism, were alarmed by reports of his visions, and within a matter of weeks Ravaillac was asked to leave. Undeterred, he attempted to join the Jesuits, but was rejected on the grounds that he had already belonged to another order. In a last attempt to gain admittance, he described his mystical visions. The Jesuit brother, seeming to interpret their true cause, gently recommended that he should eat a proper meal and get a good night's sleep. By all accounts Ravaillac's direct contact with the Jesuits had been fleeting at best, but this alleged connection would be examined repeatedly during his trial.

Having been rejected by two religious orders, Ravaillac went into a period of decline, spending a brief spell in prison – possibly for debt – that would have done nothing to improve his mental health. In 1609 he made the first of several journeys to Paris on foot with the aim of gaining an audience with Henri. Under interrogation, he would later explain that he had wanted 'to give the king advice that he should bring back to the Catholic, Apostolic and Roman Church those of the so-called Reformed religion, people completely contrary to the will of God and his Church'.[7] Each of his attempts to gain access to the king was thwarted. Three times he was turned away from the Louvre by the king's guards, but such incidents only strengthened Ravaillac's resolve, proving to him that he was being persecuted for the rightness of his cause. His hallucinations intensified, and now included a recurring vision of his murdering the king; Ravaillac became convinced it was God's will that he rid France of a tyrant. By the end of 1609 the idea was firmly rooted in his mind, and he travelled to Paris around Christmas for that very purpose, but once more he was rebuffed by the king's footmen as he approached Henri's carriage. For a brief while the obsession seems to have left him, but in early 1610 Ravaillac was once again in the capital. This time he purchased a knife, but damaged the blade before he could carry out the deed. On 14 May of that year, circumstances seemed to conspire in his favour. As the royal carriage was held up on the Rue de la Ferronnerie, Ravaillac struck, stabbing the king.

In the panic that followed, Ravaillac made no attempt to flee. He was swiftly arrested and for his own safety taken to the nearby Hôtel de Retz to avoid lynching by an outraged mob, and later transferred to the Conciergerie. Almost immediately, rumours of witchcraft began to circulate. According to the diarist Pierre Lestoile, a search of his person had revealed 'characters and instruments of sorcery, including a heart pierced in three places'.[8] In the 17th century 'characters' were talismans or symbols purported to have magical powers. According to Ravaillac's own confession, he believed he was acting in God's name, and his visions, although clearly an indication of a disturbed mental state, were religious in nature, so in all likelihood this suspicion of sorcery was an early attempt to make sense of a seemingly senseless act. In an age when superstition and belief in the supernatural were as much a part of the fabric of life as one's faith in God, witchcraft offered a seemingly comprehensible explanation and reinforced Ravaillac's role as a perpetrator of unnatural acts. It also confirmed him as a sinner almost beyond redemption (in 17th-century eyes, even Protestants had a hope of conversion), at the same time neatly side-stepping the possibility that the king's death might have been politically motivated.

This explanation did not convince many for long, however. The nobility in particular found it inconceivable that such a pathetic figure – particularly one of such lowly status – could have been capable of carrying out so significant an act without assistance. They were convinced that Ravaillac had acted on behalf of more powerful figures, and various theories began to circulate. The issue of religion was ever present, and many believed that a group of Catholic nobles was behind the murder. Some would always remain suspicious of Henri's conversion to Catholicism: his issuing of the Edict of Nantes in 1598, which granted rights to Huguenots, and his active backing of the Netherlands against Spain seemed to indicate where his true allegiances lay. Then there was the duc d'Épernon, a prominent member of the court who had been with Henri in his carriage at the time of the murder. Had he done all he could to protect the king? It was well known that he wanted to become constable of France, and Henri's death may have helped him in his ambition. The duke had also negotiated for Marie de' Medici, Henri's second wife after the annulment of his childless marriage to Marguerite de Valois, to be accepted as regent; was this for his own political ends? Adding to the intrigue was Henri's picaresque private life. Over the course of his reign he had taken several mistresses, by whom he had fathered at least eleven children in addition to the six he had had with Marie de' Medici. One of these mistresses, Henriette d'Entragues, came under suspicion when she claimed to have a signed promise from the king affirming their son's legitimacy. If such a document were true, she stood to become mother to the heir to the throne after Henri's death – ample compensation for her bitter disappointment at not having married the king herself.

But such tales of intrigue were not surprising: bitter rivalries and petty jealousies were rife at Henri's court, and poisoning one's adversary was seen as a legitimate way of furthering one's own interests. In fact, the country seemed to have been waiting for the king's assassination. In the days leading up to the murder, rumours spread as far away as Lille, Antwerp and Cologne that Henri would die suddenly, and soon. Some even read one of Nostradamus's many gnomic utterances as a

Nostradamus reveals the future to Catherine de' Medici. The infamous seer is alleged to have foretold the St Bartholomew's Day Massacre, the marriage between Marie de' Medici and Henri IV, and the king's assassination.

portent of the king's violent death. It should be remembered, however, that Henri had been instrumental in restoring peace to France after decades of religious war, and many feared that, if he were to die, the country would be plunged back into conflict. In this context, the peculiarly prescient rumours of Henri's imminent demise can be seen as an indication of public anxiety rather than as part of a wider plot.

Despite the efforts of his interrogators, who were, according to the custom of the day, merciless in their methods, Ravaillac never wavered from his story. Torture was considered a legitimate part of the judicial process, and suspects were subject to inconceivable levels of pain. Throughout his ordeal, Ravaillac refused to admit to a wider conspiracy: he and he alone had planned and carried out the king's murder. He repeatedly returned to the issue of Henri's lenient treatment of the Huguenots, and to his belief that Henri was preparing to wage war on the pope. To fight the pope, God's representative on earth, was to wage war against God himself, Ravaillac explained; for Henri to expect his soldiers to comply was the action of a tyrant. If Ravaillac did not remove the tyrant, he would have failed in his duty to God.

On 27 May 1610 the Parlement of Paris issued its verdict. Ravaillac was 'guilty in fact and law of the crime of high treason to God and man, principally on account of the most wicked, abominable, and detestable parricide committed on the person of our late King Henri IV'.[9] Ravaillac's punishment would include a very public display of penitence, followed by a public execution of excruciating brutality in the Place de Grève (now Place de l'Hôtel de Ville). He was to be taken in a cart to the main door of Notre Dame cathedral, where he would stand, according to the sentence, 'in a long shirt, holding a lighted candle two pounds in weight, and will state publicly and unequivocally that he did maliciously and feloniously commit the aforesaid … parricide and did kill his sovereign lord with two knife wounds in the body, for which he repents and asks forgiveness of God, the King, and the Law'.[10]

On the day of the execution, a carnival atmosphere prevailed; in front of the cathedral a riotous mob interrupted Ravaillac's confession. Fearing that the crowd would complete the work of the executioner, officials hastily transferred him to the Place de Grève, the city's place of execution. A scaffold awaited the condemned man, but he would have to endure several hours of public torture before the release of death. His executioners were anxious that the king's assassin should, in the words of his sentence, feel 'his soul trickle away drop by drop', and sought to prolong the ordeal. Such an extravagant display of punishment and justice would serve both as a warning and as spectacle, offering a kind of collective catharsis. The punishment of the prisoner was not only physical: the elaborate rituals of torture that led up to the execution had a symbolic significance. It was important that the prisoner and the watching public should never be allowed to forget the eternal suffering he would endure after death. His right arm, which had wielded the murder weapon, was plunged into molten lead. In part, this was because of a contemporary belief that it was possible for individual limbs to be possessed by demons independently of the rest of the body; it also reflected the idea that punishment should somehow reflect the crime. (In some cases the condemned man had his arm removed completely.) By committing regicide the criminal was beyond redemption, and the crowd was determined there could be no hope of salvation for him: the mob's furious roars drowned out the customary prayers for the condemned man, which could not be completed. As was common practice, the prisoner was drawn and quartered over a period of hours, his limbs pulled in four separate directions by horses, aided by the crowd who dragged on the ropes to add weight. He was, incredibly, conscious for most of the ordeal, and his final request for a 'Salve Regina' before he died was met with raucous jeers.

A contemporary account describes how, following his death, 'The entire populace, no matter what their rank, hurled themselves

Ravaillac's punishment was a symbolic and extremely brutal form of execution reserved for regicides. The ordeal was intentionally prolonged: Ravaillac's sentence stipulated that he was to feel 'his soul trickle away drop by drop'.

Henri IV's death mask, allegedly taken when his embalmed body was disinterred from the church of St-Denis during the French revolution. Despite the many attempts on his life, Henri was a much-loved king, remembered for his pragmatism, compassion and egalitarian views.

on the body with swords, knives, sticks, or anything else to hand, and began beating, hacking, and tearing at it. They snatched the limbs from the executioner, savagely chopping them and dragging them through the street.'[11] Such was the frenzied, hysterical need to annihilate the body of the king's assassin that there were accounts of a woman actually consuming parts of the body. The demonization of Ravaillac was thus complete; reduced to no more than animal flesh, he had been dehumanized beyond all redemption.

Official punishment extended to the criminal's family: Ravaillac's parents had two weeks to leave France and risked hanging if they ever returned, while the family home was burnt to the ground. His other relatives were forbidden from ever using the name 'Ravaillac' again. There was never any suggestion that they had been aware of his intentions, let alone assisted in any way, but it was a commonly held belief that the family had collective responsibility for the actions of its members. The transgressions of this particular family, therefore, made its future existence impossible.

Despite attempts, both at the time and by later historians, to link Ravaillac with a wider conspiracy, it is now generally believed that he acted alone. And with four centuries' hindsight, his behaviour bears all the hallmarks of the modern assassin. Today we are all too familiar with the figure of the socially isolated misfit who has an almost messianic belief in the righteousness of his or her act – it has become a cliché that almost prevents further investigation or analysis. But Ravaillac's contemporaries would have been unfamiliar with this archetype. It thus made sense for Henri IV's subjects to view Ravaillac as a pawn of more powerful agencies – be they noble families, religious orders or even supernatural powers. Political murder itself was not uncommon in France: the religious wars had already claimed the lives of the Huguenot leader Gaspard de Coligny in 1572 and of Henri III in 1589. The question of the legitimacy of regicide, which had been raised in France by the theologian Jean Petit in the early 15th century, would continue to be argued and reinterpreted right up to the execution of Louis XVI during the revolution. Like John of Salisbury and other writers of the Middle Ages, Jean Petit viewed regicide through the prism of religion, arguing that it was 'lawful for any subject, without any order or command, according to moral, divine, and natural law, to kill or cause to be killed a traitor and disloyal tyrant'. In such a context, it was perhaps to be expected that his contemporaries should have seen Ravaillac as part of a larger plot rather than as an isolated individual with a murderous obsession and the power to leave his mark on history.

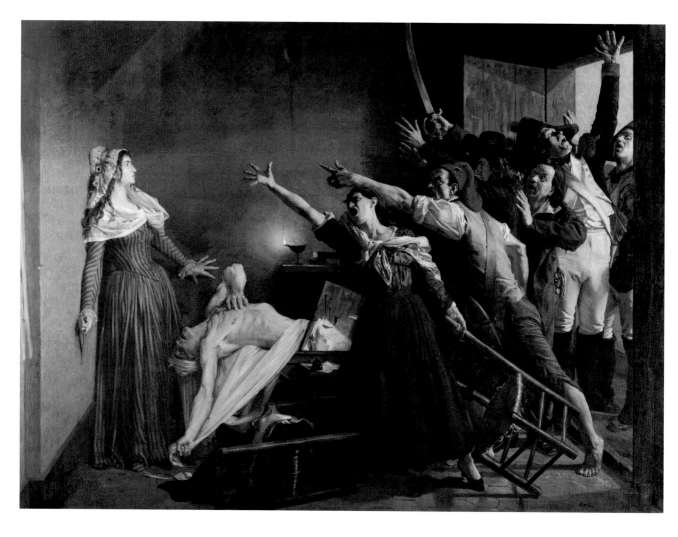

chapter 4

Martyr of the Revolution:
Jean-Paul Marat

It was the summer of 1793, and Paris had been unnaturally hot for days. Night after night, distant thunder had rumbled south-west of the capital, but no rain arrived to relieve the oppressive heat. The city was preparing for celebrations to commemorate the fall of the Bastille four years earlier; its bustling streets, festooned with decorations, were airless and rank.

On the morning of 13 July, a graceful young woman in white moved quietly among the crowd at the Palais Royal. Anyone speaking to her might have detected a Normandy accent; certainly, her clear grey eyes and fair colouring suggested northern origins. The Palais Royal was a focus for news and intrigue, and most of the city's hundreds of newspapers, periodicals and political pamphlets could be found there. The woman might have entered a *salon de lecteur* – a public reading room where, for a small fee, the latest publications could be consulted. That morning she made two small purchases: a black bonnet decorated with a green ribbon (the choice of colour would later be subject to close scrutiny), and a kitchen knife with a five-inch blade. She then proceeded to make her way across the river to the notoriously radical Cordeliers district, home and workplace of one of the revolution's most stridently polemical journalists, Jean-Paul Marat.

This scourge of counter-revolutionaries both real and alleged, and the most shrill of the revolutionary voices clamouring for reform, was a spent force. Marat's health was already poor, and he was badly affected by the summer heatwave, unable to attend the National Convention where he was a Jacobin deputy. For years he had suffered from a debilitating and disfiguring skin condition (now widely believed to have been psoriasis), which he attributed to having lived in damp basements for extended periods to avoid imprisonment for his radical publications. Now he spent the best part of each day submerged in a medicinal bath, from where he continued to write and edit his newspaper and conduct his daily business, a vinegar-soaked cloth wrapped like a turban around his thinning hair. Jacques-Louis David, the revolutionary government's minister for art and a fellow Jacobin deputy, describes a visit he made to Marat on 12 July and his shock at seeing the former firebrand's enfeebled

The assassination of the French revolutionary journalist Jean-Paul Marat in 1793, as depicted by Jean-Joseph Weerts ninety years later. The stabbing of Jean-Paul Marat by Charlotte Corday continued to fascinate painters long after the event.

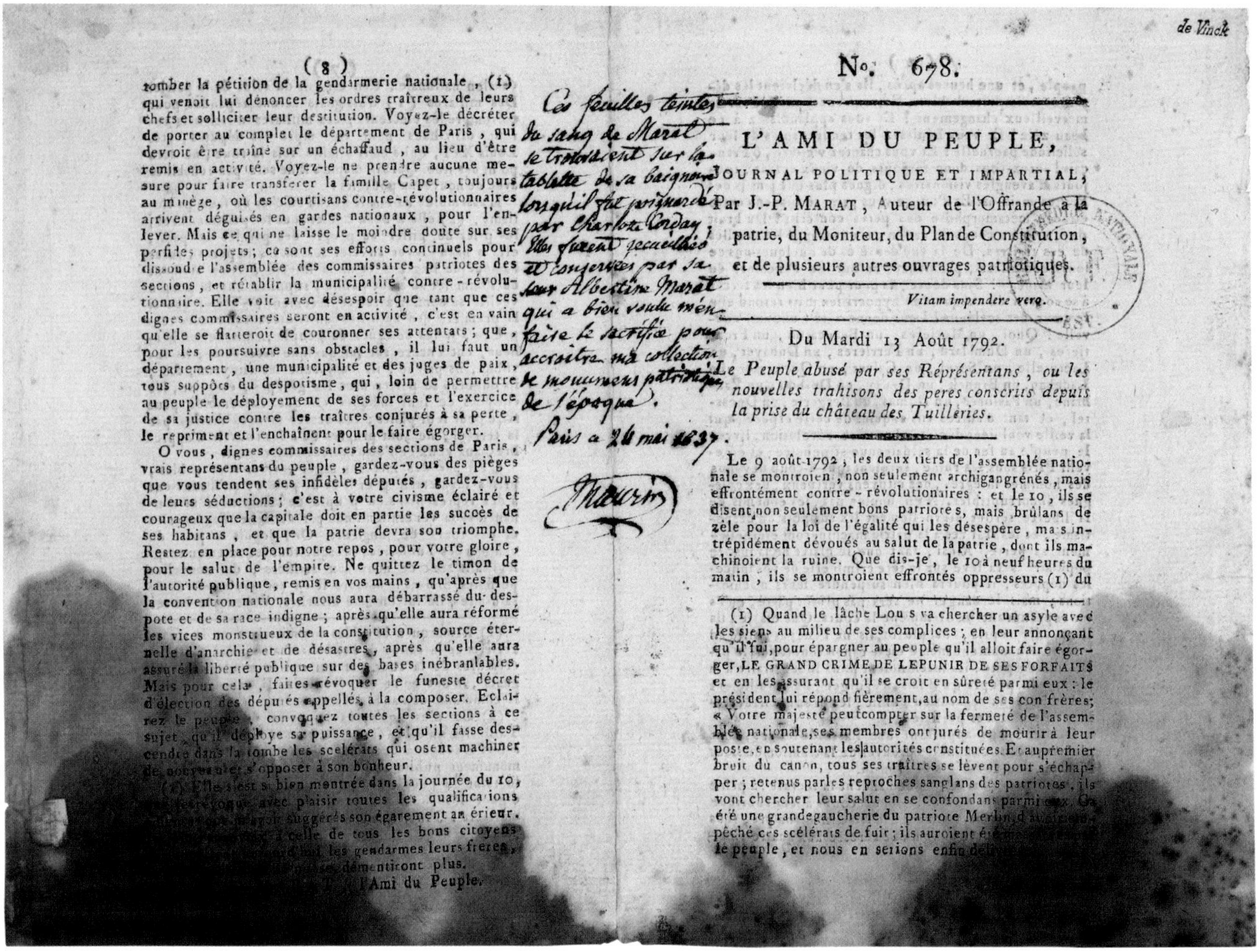

de Vinck

(8)

tomber la pétition de la gendarmerie nationale, (1) qui venoit lui dénoncer les ordres traîtreux de leurs chefs et solliciter leur destitution. Voyez-le décréter de porter au complet le département de Paris, qui devroit être traîné sur un échaffaud, au lieu d'être remis en activité. Voyez-le ne prendre aucune mesure pour faire transferer la famille Capet, toujours au manège, où les courtisans contre-révolutionnaires arrivent déguisés en gardes nationaux, pour l'enlever. Mais ce qui ne laisse le moindre doute sur ses perfides projets; ce sont ses efforts continuels pour dissoudre l'assemblée des commissaires patriotes des sections, et rétablir la municipalité contre-révolutionnaire. Elle voit avec désespoir que tant que ces dignes commissaires seront en activité, c'est en vain qu'elle se flatteroit de couronner ses attentats; que, pour les poursuivre sans obstacles, il lui faut un département, une municipalité et des juges de paix, tous suppôts du despotisme, qui, loin de permettre au peuple le déployement de ses forces et l'exercice de sa justice contre les traîtres conjurés à sa perte, le repriment et l'enchaînent pour le faire égorger.

O vous, dignes commissaires des sections de Paris, vrais représentans du peuple, gardez-vous des pièges que vous tendent ses infidèles députés, gardez-vous de leurs séductions; c'est à votre civisme éclairé et courageux que la capitale doit en partie les succès de ses habitans, et que la patrie devra son triomphe. Restez en place pour notre repos, pour votre gloire, pour le salut de l'empire. Ne quittez le timon de l'autorité publique, remis en vos mains, qu'après que la convention nationale nous aura débarrassé du despote et de sa race indigne; après qu'elle aura réformé les vices monstrueux de la constitution, source éternelle d'anarchie et de désastres, après qu'elle aura assuré la liberté publique sur des bases inébranlables. Mais pour cela, faites révoquer le funeste décret d'élection des députés appellés à la composer. Eclairez le peuple, convoquez toutes les sections à ce sujet, qu'il déploye sa puissance, et qu'il fasse descendre dans la tombe les scélérats qui osent machiner de nouveau [illegible] s'opposer à son bonheur.

(1) Elle s'est si bien montrée dans la journée du 10, [illegible] avec plaisir toutes les qualifications [illegible] suggérés son égarement antérieur. [illegible] celle de tous les bons citoyens [illegible] les gendarmes leurs freres, [illegible] démentiront plus.

[illegible] l'Ami du Peuple.

Ces feuilles teintes du sang de Marat se trouvaient sur la tablette de sa baignoire lorsqu'il fut poignardé par Charlotte Corday; elles furent recueillies et conservées par sa sœur Albertine Marat qui a bien voulu m'en faire le sacrifice pour accroître ma collection de monumens patriotiques de l'époque.

Paris a 26 mai 1837.

[signature]

No. 678.

L'AMI DU PEUPLE,

JOURNAL POLITIQUE ET IMPARTIAL,

Par J.-P. MARAT, Auteur de l'Offrande à la patrie, du Moniteur, du Plan de Constitution, et de plusieurs autres ouvrages patriotiques.

Vitam impendere vero.

Du Mardi 13 Août 1792.

Le Peuple abusé par ses Réprésentans, ou les nouvelles trahisons des peres conscrits depuis la prise du château des Tuilleries.

Le 9 août 1792, les deux tiers de l'assemblée nationale se montroient, non seulement archigangrénés, mais effrontément contre-révolutionaires : et le 10, ils se disent non seulement bons patriotes, mais brûlans de zèle pour la loi de l'égalité qui les désespère, mais intrépidément dévoués au salut de la patrie, dont ils machinoient la ruine. Que dis-je, le 10 à neuf heures du matin, ils se montroient effrontés oppresseurs (1) du

(1) Quand le lâche Louis va chercher un asyle avec les siens au milieu de ses complices; en leur annonçant qu'il fui, pour épargner au peuple qu'il alloit faire égorger, LE GRAND CRIME DE LE PUNIR DE SES FORFAITS et en les assurant qu'il se croit en sûreté parmi eux : le président lui répond fièrement, au nom de ses con frères; « Votre majesté peut compter sur la fermeté de l'assemblée nationale, ses membres ont jurés de mourir à leur poste, en soutenant les autorités constituées. Et au premier bruit du canon, tous ses traitres se lèvent pour s'échapper; retenus par les reproches sanglans des patriotes, ils vont chercher leur salut en se confondans parmi eux. Ça été une grande gaucherie du patriote Merlin, d'avoir empêché ces scélérats de fuir; ils auroient [illegible] le peuple, et nous en serions enfin [illegible]

A copy of L'Ami du peuple *('The People's Friend'), Marat's revolutionary newspaper, stained with his own blood during Corday's attack. Of the many political newspapers published in Paris at the time, Marat's was the most vitriolic, urging violence in the name of revolution.*

appearance: 'I found him in a state which stunned me. Beside him was a wooden box on which there was an inkwell and paper, and with his hand out of the bath he was writing his final thoughts for the deliverance of his people.'[1]

David's dismay was understandable: Marat's journalistic and political career was remarkable for its vitality and vituperative energy. Since the beginning of the revolution Marat had written, edited and published pamphlets, placards and a daily newspaper almost continuously, stopping only for brief periods when his blend of bloodthirsty rabble-rousing and shrill invective had led to warrants for his arrest and forced him, at times literally, underground. *L'Ami du peuple* was not only the name of his most popular, and most notorious, publication: it had also become his moniker. It was as the 'People's Friend' that Marat had made his name as a Jacobin deputy, issuing a seemingly unstoppable barrage of invective denouncing the revolution's enemies at the same time as championing the cause of the people. His rhetorical style in the Convention matched that of his prose – bombastic, accusatory and fanatical. Of the voices calling for the new republic to be purged of traitors through the cleansing blade of the guillotine, Marat's was among the loudest.

Like many during this extraordinary period, Jean-Paul Marat (1743–93) had been made by the revolution. Prior to finding his journalistic voice he had had a career in medicine, working for some years in the household of the king's brother, the comte d'Artois, and even gaining a noble benefactress – one marquise de Laubespine – after he appeared to have cured her of tuberculosis. Nonetheless, Marat felt that he had never achieved the recognition that was his due. Although he had published in the fields of optics, light and electricity with some degree of success (Benjamin Franklin had attended a public demonstration of one of his experiments), he was never accepted into the prestigious Academy of Sciences – an oversight he resented all his life. (Indeed, it is possible that Marat's pursuit of certain figures was the result of personal rivalry. Jean-Sylvain Bailly, for instance – who was mayor of Paris until his execution, and the target of Marat's endless spleen – had been a member of the Academy.) Marat's reputation as a physician was not helped when his patented cure for tuberculosis was discovered to be nothing more than powdered chalk and water.

The dramatic events of 1789, however, showed Marat his true vocation. Nearly a decade spent in England had exposed him to the radical journalism of the likes of John Wilkes, and Marat's combative, hectoring prose, heavy with sarcasm, was informed by the style of these English radicals. In one of many self-mythologizing accounts, Marat described how reports of the coming revolution had literally brought him back from the brink of death, forcing him to rouse himself to fight for the new ideals of Liberty, Equality and Fraternity. He recalled hearing the news of the meeting of the Estates-General in 1789, a truly historic gathering that had last taken place in 1614:

> I was on my deathbed when a friend, the only person I wanted by
> my side to witness my last moments, told me about the convocation
> of the Estates-General. The news had a powerful effect on me;
> my illness broke and my spirits revived.[2]

This momentous occurrence was an attempt by Louis XVI to address the country's impending bankruptcy, the result of the revolutionary war it was waging in America. The Estates-General was a quasi-parliamentary body comprising the aristocracy (the First Estate), the clergy (the Second Estate) and the 'people' (the Third Estate), who were delegates from local assemblies. It had

This engraving shows the different stages of Marat's life: his time as a physician, selling his patented cures; as hero of the revolution, borne aloft in triumph after his successful acquittal at a Paris tribunal; and, following his brief apotheosis, a final fall from grace, when his busts were removed and broken into pieces.

François Gérard, 10 August 1792: The Crowd Invades the Assembly, *c. 1795. On 10 August 1792, Parisian sans-culottes stormed the Tuileries Palace, the residence of the king, and proceeded to rampage through Paris destroying all symbols of monarchy.*

last convened under Louis XIV, and its reappearance marked the beginning of a seemingly unstoppable chain of events that led France from monarchy to republic.

Marat's recollection of the Estates-General is characteristic of his journalism, in which political upheavals are mirrored by personal drama. Inspired by the momentousness of the occasion, the former Dr Marat, physician to the aristocracy, reissued an anonymous pamphlet he had written entitled *Offrande à la patrie* ('An Offering to the Nation'), proposing to the delegates of the Third Estate a series of political reforms. It was considerably more moderate than his later publications, and at this early stage of the revolution none of the would-be reformers was agitating for the end of the monarchy ('the enemies of the nation … howl for innovations and the overthrow of the monarchy … we are not innovators; we have no desire whatsoever to overthrow the throne'[3]). Marat's early tract was part of a great mass of material being printed in response to current events, and as such it attracted little attention. As the revolution gathered momentum, however, Marat would find his voice, his supporters – and his enemies. From the outset, his attitude was one of vehement righteousness, and he seemed to take a perverse pride in inspiring animosity in high places. He considered truth the highest of virtues, unpalatable only to those who had something to hide. As time went on, he pointed to the number of enemies he had made as evidence of his rightness, as if enmity itself gave his opinions credibility. Seeming all too eager to reject the privileged milieu in which he had once moved, Marat wrote how 'My friends raised the very devil with me to try stop me from writing about current events, but I just let them howl and wasn't afraid to lose them.'[4] Later, in 1793, he wrote: 'To pretend to please everyone is mad, but to pretend to please everyone in a time of revolution is treason.'[5] As the upheaval progressed, he would make his career identifying and denouncing such alleged acts of treason, his hectoring accusations often provoking counter-claims of libel. He was always the first to point the finger at perceived hypocrisy, singling out heroes of the early revolution – among them General Lafayette and Louis's popular finance minister Jacques Necker – for particularly vicious attacks.

Marat's specific brand of patriotic fervour and vitriol soon attracted a loyal following among the working people of Paris, whom he would champion all his life. He claimed: 'It is the class of citizens with the least fortune that is the only one that is patriotic, just as it is the only honest one.'[6] After a few early attempts at publishing a daily paper, Marat found his stride with the publication of *L'Ami du peuple*, in September 1789. The relaxing of press restrictions and developments in print technology contributed to a rich culture of popular publications, and daily newspapers such as Jacques-René Hébert's *sans-culotte* organ *Le Père Duchesne*, or Marat's own, or were read avidly in revolutionary clubs. At its height, Marat's *L'Ami du peuple* ran to a couple of thousand copies a day –

The French revolution saw a flood of printed material of all kinds. Bought and sold with great enthusiasm, it introduced the radical ideas of journalists such as Marat to a wider public. This drawing of a pamphlet-seller, by Philibert-Louis Debucourt, dates to 1791, 'Year Three of Liberty'.

a staggering number for its time – and since newspapers were shared, or read aloud in clubs and cafés, his readership was probably three to four times that number. At times of political crisis, Marat did away with his newspaper altogether and issued his pronouncements as placards, providing commentary on events almost as they unfolded. Turbulent times inspire passionate language, but Marat's reached new levels of bombast. Some have suggested that his writing was not intended to be taken literally, that his bloodiest announcements were metaphorical. This is highly unlikely. Marat was acutely aware of his readership. He wrote for the *sans-culottes*, the often illiterate working men and women of Paris who gathered their news in the city's workshops, wine shops, street corners and revolutionary clubs. For the first time in France's history they had a voice and a political presence, and they were seen as the true heroes of the revolution. They were accustomed to calls to arms, not rhetorical flourishes, and would have taken at face value texts such as the following:

> *Five or six hundred heads chopped off would assure you peace, liberty,*
> *and happiness … Let your enemies triumph for an instant and torrents*
> *of blood will flow. They'll cut your throats without mercy, they'll slit*
> *the bellies of your wives, and in order to forever extinguish your love*
> *of liberty, their bloody hands will reach into your children's entrails*
> *and rip their hearts out.*
>
> – *L'Ami du peuple*, 27 May 1791[7]

Although he was not alone in calling for mass executions, Marat was certainly among the most vociferous, and he undeniably had the ear of the people. As the tumbrels made their way to the guillotine, Marat's voice was increasingly influential, even prophetic. 'Cassandra Marat', his fellow Jacobin and journalist Camille Desmoulins would call him, as many of Marat's warnings and predictions of counter-revolutionary plots appeared to come true.

Yet was this apparent gift for prophecy in fact a form of covert incitement? Marat's increasing number of enemies seemed to think so. By the spring of 1793 he had become more actively involved in revolutionary politics, acting as a deputy in the Convention and then as Secretary of the Committee of Surveillance. He was aligned with the radical Jacobins known as the 'Montagnards' ('the Mountain' – so-called because they sat high up in the benches of the National Assembly), who included among their the number Desmoulins and Danton. In time, even the Mountain would find Marat's invective and accusations an embarrassment, but now they took advantage of his success in goading the more moderate Girondin faction. It was the Girondists, hoping to stem the bloody tide that the revolution had unleashed, who were anxious of Marat's power to incite violence. They still recalled with horror the events of September 1792 and questioned the extent of Marat's involvement.

On 25 July 1792 the duke of Brunswick had pledged the support of Austria and Prussia in restoring Louis to the throne. The situation in Paris was already extremely volatile, and by late August more than 1,000 people had been arrested and imprisoned for supposed counter-revolutionary activities. These arrests were based on the faintest of pretexts, and those apprehended included priests, servants, courtiers and journalists. In such an atmosphere no one was above suspicion. The idea of eternal vigilance – of the need to be ever watchful for enemies of the republic – was a continuous feature of the revolutionaries' language, and citizens were encouraged to denounce neighbours, colleagues and even family members.

When news reached Paris that Prussian forces had crossed into France, the very real threat of the army marching on the capital only worsened the general hysteria and sense of fear and mistrust. As the city was emptied of able-bodied men joining the French army, rumours spread that invading Prussians would liberate prisoners (the prisons were believed to harbour counter-revolutionaries) and join with them in taking over the capital. On 2 September, news arrived that Verdun, the last fortified town on the road to Paris, had fallen to the enemy.

A woodcut depicting the atrocities of the September Massacres, in which thousands of prisoners, including children, were executed by a mob that accused them of counter-revolutionary activities. Zealots like Marat contributed to the atmosphere of fear and vengeance.

In response, the *sans-culottes* began to put on trial and execute prisoners, at first with the notion of eradicating fifth columnists who might collude with the army. Soon all pretence of a tribunal was abandoned and the prisoners – among them aristocrats, clergy, common criminals, prostitutes, beggars and children – were dragged from their cells into the prison courtyards and beaten, stoned or bayoneted by frenzied mobs, many of whom celebrated long into the night, dancing drunkenly around open fires. The princesse de Lamballe, the former favourite of Marie Antoinette, was beaten unconscious and eviscerated, her head paraded on a pike to the window at the Temple prison where the queen herself was imprisoned. When the carnage ended four days later, 1,400 people – half the prison population of Paris – were dead.

Marat's role in the September Massacres has been the subject of a great deal of debate. Certainly, after the fall of Robespierre, in the immediate post-Thermidor period, he was seen by anti-Jacobins to have been the prime instigator of the episode. At a time when dramatic power shifts saw figures who had been deified one day vilified the next, the demonization of Marat was only to be expected as the Jacobins fell from power. The day the massacres began, he had become a member of the Committee of Surveillance, the body established by the revolutionary government expressly to expose counter-revolutionary activity. A month after the massacres, he had insisted that the committee had ordered the common prisoners to be separated from the counter-revolutionaries. And yet, in the weeks that led up to the attacks, Marat had asked the people to 'rise and let the blood of traitors flow again'; the death of convicts in the Abbaye prison was 'the only means of saving the Fatherland'.[8] The extent to which Marat was responsible for the massacres in an official capacity is probably limited, but in his role as a journalist he undeniably contributed to the atmosphere of fear and suspicion that allowed them to occur.

Marat's reputation clearly preceded him when he made his first appearance as a Jacobin deputy at the Convention in September 1792. The moderate Girondins sat on the right of the Convention, while the radical Mountain (the Montagnards) sat high up on benches on the left-hand side. (This arrangement, established during the Estates-General, gives us the political terms 'right wing' and 'left wing'.) Between the two sat 'the Plain' – the deputies with no party, who needed to be won over by either side to secure their vote. When Marat first appeared in the Convention, many of the moderates were surprised to discover that 'L'Ami du peuple' was in fact a real person, having imagined him to be nothing more than a Jacobin bogeyman, the product of the radicals'

fanatical imaginations. He clearly looked the part, rejecting, in the
manner of the true revolutionary, any semblance of fastidiousness,
which was increasingly associated with loyalty to the aristocracy.
('He dressed in a careless manner [which] one might almost say gave him
an air of uncleanliness,' wrote a fellow Jacobin in an otherwise admiring
tribute.[9]) True to form, Marat seemed to welcome the hostile reaction
to his arrival in the Convention. Amid boos and catcalls he made his first
speech, acknowledging the 'great number of personal enemies in this
assembly'. When a Girondin deputy reminded the Convention that
there was an outstanding warrant for Marat's arrest for seditious writing,
and accused him of having blood on his hands, Marat's response was
as dramatic in person as it would have been on the page: he pulled a
pistol from his waistband, waved it at his head and threatened to blow
out his brains if there were any truth in the accusation. Wild cheers
erupted from the *sans-culottes* in the public gallery, who supported all his
appearances, characterized by dramatic rhetoric or an eye for the grand

LE TRIOMPHE DE MARAT.

Il se qualifioit L'ami du Peuple, et par ses écrits il les excitoit à être pillard et assassin, disant qu'il falloit tuer 2 à 300 mille hommes, prendre le bien des Riches, et des Marchands, et le partager entre le Peuple, ce qui plaisoit beaucoup à la populace. Il fut dénoncé comme ayant reçu de l'argent de la faction d'Orléans, il fut arrêté, et mis en Jugement; mais les Jacobins ne voulant pas perdre, leur plus zélé partisan, le firent déclarer innocent. Le Peuple l'emporta de la Salle d'audience, et le promena en Triomphe, jusqu'à la convention. Cela le rendit plus hardis a publier ses dangereuses opinions, Jusqu'à ce qu'il fut assassiné. Comme on sait. 8.bre.

Marat's appearance and swift acquittal at the Revolutionary Tribunal became part of French revolutionary lore. He was crowned with laurel and borne aloft by a cheering crowd. Gouache by the Le Sueur brothers, 1793.

gesture. His denunciation of the aristocratic military hero General Dumouriez was carefully orchestrated to take place at a private party in the general's honour at one of Paris's more fashionable addresses. Barging into the select gathering in full firebrand mode, a mangy fur scarf flung over his shoulders, he and two Jacobins accosted Dumouriez and accused him of planning to defect to the Austrians. (Six months later 'Cassandra Marat' would be proven right.) Once Marat and his friends had left, one wit pointedly sprayed the air with perfume, to remove the stench, both literal and metaphorical, of Jacobinism.

Although Marat was increasingly identified with the Jacobins, they did not universally like him. Danton, originally a supporter, had fallen out with him over the September Massacres, declaring to the Convention that he did not 'like the individual Marat … He is not only volcanic and bitter, but unsociable';[10] and Robespierre the Incorruptible abandoned him to the hostility of the Girondins in Convention debates. Many feared that his extremism would alienate the central Plain and sought to reject him from the Jacobin Club. Yet as the revolution become more and more extreme, Marat's star continued to rise. He joined in the call for king's death in January 1793, and was instrumental in implementing a system of oral voting for the execution (all the easier to identify enemies of the republic). By April 1793 he had become president of the Jacobins – only a temporary position, but nonetheless evidence of his high standing. At this point the Girondins made their last attempt to remove Marat. With many Jacobin deputies on missions in the provinces, the Girondins took advantage of a depleted Convention to gather examples of Marat's texts denouncing leading Girondins as royalist accomplices and accusing them of fomenting civil war. 'The counter-revolution is in the government, in the National Convention! That's where it has to be smashed! Arise, republican!'[11] Those few who were present voted for his arrest.

As a journalist, Marat had spent a great deal of his career evading the police; he now waited three days before turning himself in amid great fanfare and wild popular support. When he appeared in court, the spectators erupted in cheers; he had to request their silence before he could present his defence. Marat's eloquent speech, coupled with a sympathetic prosecutor and judge, led to a swift acquittal. He was carried from the courtroom in triumph, the laurel wreath of the Roman victor crowning his head. A victory celebration held at the Jacobin Club some days later was so well attended that a stand collapsed under the weight of his cheering supporters.

Pierre-Alexandre Wille, Charlotte Corday in Prison, *1793. Corday's youth, beauty and gender were as fascinating to revolutionary Paris as her crime was repellent. A witness to her execution, a young German republican named Adam Lux, was so moved by the sight of her that he wrote a pamphlet denouncing the Revolutionary Tribunal and was shortly afterwards executed.*

The Girondins came out worst from the affair: their persecution of Marat served only to consolidate his position as the people's hero at the same time as seeming to confirm the truth of his accusations. After all, Marat had predicted that the Girondin-supported General Dumouriez would emigrate to Austria, which had duly happened earlier in April. The trial's outcome illustrated how far the *sans-culottes* feared and mistrusted the Girondins. Over the coming weeks thirty-one leading Girondins, as well as the former *sans-culotte* favourite Jacques Hébert, were arrested. He and twenty-one others were guillotined in October 1793.

Of the Girondins who were able to escape Paris, Charles Jean Marie Barbaroux, a vociferous opponent of Marat, fled to Caen in Normandy (a recognized centre of counter-revolutionary sentiment). It was from here that he and his supporters began to organize a Girondin rebellion, publicly denouncing the radical Jacobins in Paris and accusing Marat in particular of perverting the cause of Liberty, promoting a revolutionary dictatorship and destroying republican freedoms.

Profoundly impressed by these impassioned speeches was a young woman named Charlotte Corday, the daughter of Norman gentry and a descendant of the 17th-century dramatist Pierre Corneille. Corday had had the benefit of a classical education, studying Plutarch among others, and was deeply influenced by Rousseau and other heroes of the Enlightenment. She would have been familiar with Classical debates on the subject of tyrannicide, particularly those raised in Plutarch's *Life of Caesar*. Inspired by the Girondins' speeches, Corday came to identify Marat as the demon who was destroying her beloved France, holding him solely responsible for the bloody excesses of the revolution and for the September Massacres in particular. She would later cite the heroes of antiquity as her inspiration, comparing herself to Brutus in her willingness to sacrifice herself for the good of her country. The unprecedented participation of women in direct political action (and violence) during the revolution may have also played its part in Charlotte Corday's decision to make the journey to Paris. High-profile revolutionary women such as Olympe de Gouges or Théroigne de Méricourt (known as 'l'Amazone'), as well as the female-dominated October March on Versailles in 1789, proved that women had an active part to play in the forging of the new republic.

Charlotte Corday arrived in the capital on 11 July 1793. Her plan was to assassinate Marat in public, in the Convention, surrounded by deputies. She had no intention of evading capture. It was only when she heard that he was too ill to appear that she revised her plan and decided to approach him at home. On 13 July, having bought a knife and a new hat decorated with green ribbon (the colour of liberty promoted by Camille Desmoulins in the early days of the revolution – or was it the colour of royalist livery?), she arrived at Marat's door, only to be turned away by his fiancée's sister, who claimed he was too ill to receive visitors – even pretty young women claiming to have important information for him.

Corday returned to her lodgings, where, in the hope of gaining access to Marat, she wrote and dispatched a letter claiming to be able to provide the names of counter-revolutionary Girondists plotting in Caen. When she received no reply, she wrote another appealing to Marat's sense of duty to the downtrodden, pleading: 'I am persecuted for the cause of liberty. I am unhappy; this itself is sufficient to give me a claim on your protection.'[12] She also drafted a speech to the French people; in the event that she might not live to stand trial, she wanted her motives to be made public. This she pinned to her dress, along with her baptism certificate, before returning to Marat's house that evening. Again she was turned away, but this time was able to take advantage of a delivery

Jean-Jacques Hauer's depiction of Marat's murder, painted in 1794, is entirely different from David's idealized version (see p. 88). The peculiar shoe-shaped bath is nonetheless completely accurate. Hauer sketched Corday when she was in prison, a request granted to her by the Revolutionary Tribunal.

to gain entry to the house. Stopped on the stairs by Simonne, Marat's fiancée, Charlotte raised her voice sufficiently for Marat to hear her from his bath. 'Let her come in,' he called, and Charlotte Corday was ushered in to see the People's Friend.

Was she shocked by the frail and sickly figure before her? Immersed in his bath, wearing a soaked dressing gown and damp turban, the ogre of the revolution must have presented a pathetic sight. A wooden board lay across the bath, on which were scattered his many papers and letters. Corday drew near, reeling off a list of eighteen Girondin deputies alleged to be involved in counter-revolutionary activities in Caen. Marat nodded: 'It will not be long before they're guillotined,' he said. Then, with surprising ease, she plunged her knife in just above his collarbone, severing a main artery and puncturing his lung. Marat cried out to Simonne, who entered the room screaming, alerting those who lived nearby. Marat died within minutes, and Corday, after a half-hearted attempt to evade capture, was held by the householders and excited neighbours until the arrival of the police, who took her to the Abbaye prison. At her trial before the revolutionary Tribunal, held four days later, Corday admitted her guilt at once: 'All these details are needless. It is I who killed Marat … I killed one man to save a hundred thousand; a villain to save innocents; a savage wild-beast to give repose to my country. I was a Republican before the Revolution; I never wanted energy.'[13] Among the spectators at the trial was a young German academic, Adam Lux, who, beguiled by her bravery and beauty, was later to compare her to Brutus. He was guillotined for his admiration.

Charlotte Corday was taken to the guillotine on the day of her trial, standing upright in the jolting tumbrel despite having her hands bound behind her back. Her hair was crudely shorn at the nape of her neck, and she wore the blood-red shirt of the murderer. Witnesses

Charlotte Corday being led to the guillotine, 17 July 1793. Contemporary accounts describe her lack of fear and her dignified bearing, despite the jolts of the tumbrel and the fact that her hands were tied behind her back. She wore the red shirt reserved for assassins of 'representatives of the people'.

Jean-Paul Marat's funeral in the church of the Cordeliers. The highly ritualized obsequies, devised by minister of culture Jacques-Louis David, were specifically designed to transform Marat into a republican martyr (note the bathtub and wooden packing case).

described the sky darkening and torrential rain soaking the streets, and yet throughout her last journey 'her beautiful face was so calm that one would have said she was a statue'.[14] Her executioner was less enamoured of her: when he held her head aloft for the crowds – a customary part of the public spectacle of execution – he gave her cheek a resounding slap. According to legend, it blushed bright red.

Charlotte Corday had been prepared to sacrifice herself for the good of her country. Yet her bloody act halted neither the revolution nor Marat, who in death became more useful to the Jacobins than he had been alive. As one contemporary noted, 'With a single act, Charlotte Corday killed a man and created a God.' The Jacobin government needed its heroes of the revolution; it needed its symbols and secular icons. Catholic France had been stripped of its religious faith when the Jacobins had implemented a vast programme of dechristianization, closing churches, monasteries and convents, turning out the clergy and removing all vestiges of Catholic devotion from public spaces. In place of church services Robespierre orchestrated festivals that honoured the Supreme Being instead of God. The revolutionary calendar had done away with the seven-day week, in the process abolishing both Sundays and saints' days, of which there were many. But now the revolution had its own martyr to replace the venerated Christian saints.

In his role of minister of culture, Jacques-Louis David had planned an elaborate funeral in which Marat's body would lie in state, posed like a fallen Classical hero, with one arm draped over the side of his bath – just as the artist had found him the day before his assassination and would later depict him in his painting. A similarly choreographed funeral for the assassinated deputy Le Pelletier, who was stabbed by a loyalist shortly after he had voted for the king's execution, had taken place in January: the winter cold had preserved the body for the duration of the public viewing and the ceremony. In the stifling summer heat, however, Marat's body had already begun to putrefy. It was displayed for two days at the church of the Cordeliers convent (where the radical Cordeliers had first held their meetings) between 14 and 16 July, with the bathtub alongside, but it had required cosmetics to make the body presentable and liberal use of vinegar to disguise the smell of decay. On the final evening a vast funeral procession made its away around Paris; comprising the whole of the Convention, the popular revolutionary societies and many ordinary citizens, the cortège – according to *The Times* of London – 'followed the

The abolition of the Catholic church did not mean that France had become an atheist country. Robespierre concocted elaborate ceremonies to honour 'the Supreme Being', with their own symbolism and rituals. This print shows the mound erected on the Champ de la Réunion for the 'Festival of the Supreme Being' in 1794.

Du 13. Juillet, 1793.
Marie anne Charlotte
Corday au citoyen
Marat.
il Suffit que je Sois
bien Malheureuse
pour avoir Droit
à votre bienveillance

À MARAT,
DAVID.

L'AN — DEUX

opposite *Jacques-Louis David,*
The Death of Marat, c. *1794.*
One of the revolution's best-known
images, David's painting succeeds in
creating an icon of the murdered Marat.
The tools of his trade – his pen, ink
and paper – replace the symbols of the
Christian saints; and the only references
to his bloody death are the small knife
at the bottom left of the image and a
discreet cut under his collar bone.

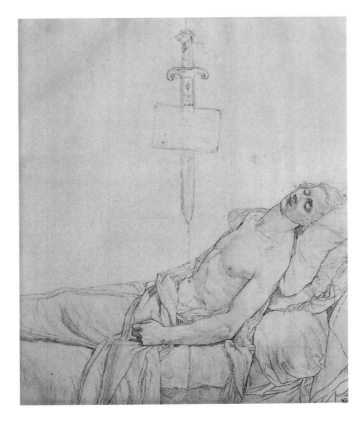

Drawing after David's Le Pelletier
de Saint-Fargeau on his Deathbed,
1793. Le Pelletier, a republican deputy
who had voted for the execution of the
king, was stabbed on 20 January 1793.
This classical depiction of Pelletier's
corpse clearly foreshadows David's
later painting.

body in profound silence to the sound of mournful music. The cannon was
fired in several quarters of the city. Marat was interred under the trees of
the garden of the Convent of Cordeliers, at two in the morning. His tomb
is a rough stone without any ornament.' The body was later moved to the
Panthéon, and his embalmed heart transferred to the Cordeliers Club.

If the veneration of Marat's body had not gone exactly to plan,
David's painting of the assassinated radical provided the revolution
with a potent and timeless symbol. In this canvas, often described as a
republican *pietà*, David has almost entirely eradicated any elements of
physical violation and decay from the serene figure of the dying Marat.
The stabbing is indicated by a discreet wound above the collarbone,
his disfiguring disease only by a small patch of discoloured skin on the
elbow. So pristine is the body, with its marble-like skin tone, that it
almost comes as a surprise to notice the red bath water. Scattered about,
like the totems of a Christian saint, are the tools of Marat's trade and
those of his murderer. The inscription – 'To Marat, David' – reinforces
the idea of the painting as an effigy. But it was not the only such image
to fulfil that role: Marat's bust appeared in public places all over France.
It was venerated in town squares and replaced the crucified Christ in
churches. On festival days, his picture would appear on banners in public

processions, and women's revolutionary clubs raised funds to create Neoclassical temples to him. Along with the child martyr Joseph Bara, killed by royalists in the Vendée uprising, Marat became a symbol of sacrifice in the name of Liberty. Four months after his death, on 16 October 1793, David's painting of Marat was displayed to the public for the first time, in the courtyard of the Louvre. That morning, in the nearby Place de la Révolution, Marie Antoinette had been taken to the guillotine in an open *charrette*, her last words an apology to the executioner for treading on his foot.

Charlotte Corday inspired her own, unofficial, cult, which, once the Jacobins had fallen from power, flourished well into the late 19th century. The potent combination of youth, beauty and self-sacrifice she represented made her a beguiling symbol for the Romantic era, and she featured in paintings, sculpture, poetry and plays long after her death. Even at the time of her execution, the *sans-culotte* crowd was outraged by the executioner's contemptuous treatment of her decapitated head. According to *The Times*, 'This was considered as such an atrocious act, that the very Tribunal who had condemned her to death, sentenced her executioner to twelve years imprisonment in irons.'[15] The consensus was that, although her crime deserved to be punished, her person demanded respect. And indeed, her comportment throughout her trial and execution suggest that she was acutely aware of her position in history. In the speech she wrote to explain her actions, she compared them to the stoical self-sacrifices of antiquity, sincerely believing that by removing Marat she would change the course of history. By making reference to Classical precedents she was able both to justify her act and to set it apart from the executions carried out by the revolutionary government in the name of the republic.

Marat's death did not have an immediate effect on the excesses of the revolution. Shortly afterwards the blood-crazed Reign of Terror was unleashed, which continued unabated for two years; more and more lives were lost to the blade of the guillotine, having been tried and found wanting by Robespierre's government. But Robespierre was increasingly isolated, and the support of his deputies in the Convention was dwindling away. On 9 Thermidor Year II (27 July 1794), Robespierre, along with other members of the Committee for Public Safety, was arrested by a faction of rebel Montagnards and executed without trial the next day. Without Charlotte Corday, Marat would very likely have been among them. The execution of the most radical members of the revolutionary government ended the Terror, ushering in a more moderate regime and paving the way for the Directory government of November 1795.

chapter 5

Anarchy, Nationalism and the Black Hand: *Archduke Franz Ferdinand*

Sunday 28 June 1914 was bathed in sunshine, a day of radiant blue and gold. The buildings lining Sarajevo's Appel Quay were festooned with flags and flowers to celebrate the visit of the Habsburg heir, Archduke Franz Ferdinand, and his wife, Sophie. Excited onlookers lined the streets, awaiting the arrival of the motorcade. The riverbed running alongside the quay was nearly dry in the summer heat, and only a few inches of water passed beneath the three bridges that spanned the Miljačka river. As the column of cars approached the quay, the crowds began to cheer. In the first vehicle sat the mayor and the police commissioner of Sarajevo, immediately followed by an open-topped car, its Habsburg flag fluttering in the wind, that carried the archduke, his wife and General Potiorek, governor of Bosnia.[1] Two more cars came on behind, laden with members of the royal entourage and local dignitaries. As they moved along the quay, two young men, little more than youths, were standing next to the Čumurja Bridge. One fumbled in his pocket, then seemed to hesitate, standing motionless as his cohort hurled a small metal object at the second vehicle. A sharp noise rang out, like the sound of a car backfiring; the driver of the third vehicle, assuming he had a flat tyre, slowed almost to a halt, but the archduke's chauffeur accelerated and the object – a bomb – bounced off the car into the road. After several seconds it exploded, injuring several onlookers as well as the governor's aide-de-camp, Colonel Merizzi, who was travelling in the vehicle behind, while the detonating cap grazed the duchess's neck. The young man by the bridge, fearing arrest, attempted to escape by jumping into the river. He was almost immediately apprehended and taken to the police station. The motorcade then continued its stately way to the town hall, as planned. The archduke, less fearful than furious, and in a show of temper for which he was notorious, turned on the mayor as he attempted to begin his speech: 'Mr Mayor, I come here on a visit and I get bombs thrown at me. It is outrageous.' Having expressed his fury, he continued: 'Now you may speak.'[2]

After a brief consultation, it was decided to abandon the official programme of events, which on the previous two days had included military inspections; the entourage would instead make its way to the

Nedeljko Čabrinović (left) and Gavrilo Princip (right) receiving instruction from Milan Ciganović of the Black Hand, the Serbian nationalist group involved in the assassination plot against Archduke Franz Ferdinand. Photographed in Belgrade, in the spring of 1914.

93

Sunday 28 June 1914: Having completed
his speech, Archduke Franz Ferdinand
and his wife, Duchess Sophie, leave
Sarajevo town hall.

train station at the first opportunity. It has been suggested that this decision was less out of fear of further attacks on the archduke's life than a form of reprimand to the city of Sarajevo for the outrage committed against him. Franz Ferdinand, however, refused to leave before visiting the wounded Merizzi in hospital, and thus the motorcade began its fateful trip back down Appel Quay – a street that the archbishop of Sarajevo would later describe as 'a regular avenue of assassins'.[3] For, in addition to the two young men standing on Čumurja Bridge, another four co-conspirators had been positioned along the Appel Quay route. All but Nedeljko Čabrinović had lost their nerve as the car had passed, and after his failed bomb attack had melted into the crowd. The first attempt on the archduke's life had failed because of human error; the second would succeed for the same reason.

Since the official procession route had been well publicized, it was decided to drive back along the quay to the garrison hospital, the logic being that no one would expect them to pass that way twice. This time, however, Count Franz von Harrach, who previously had been a passenger in the archduke's car, positioned himself on the left-hand running board to shield the royal couple from any further attacks. The line of cars (minus the damaged vehicle) began to retrace its journey down the quay; it was headed by the police commissioner, as

Franz Ferdinand's car on Appel Quay moments before the assassination.

Princip takes aim at Archduke Franz
Ferdinand and his wife in Sarajevo:
an engraving from the Italian newspaper
La Domenica del Corriere.

before, with General Potiorek and the royal visitors behind. But there seemed to be some confusion over the route: for an unknown reason the driver of the first vehicle turned right at the Lateiner Bridge into Franz Joseph Strasse, a narrow street lined with cafés, and the second car followed. Realizing that there had been error, Potiorek ordered the chauffeur to reverse back onto Appel Quay. At this point, as the car was at a standstill, a young man approached from the right and fired two shots, hitting the archduke in the jugular vein and the duchess in the abdomen. A thin stream of blood hit Harrach on the cheek, and the duchess collapsed into the archduke's lap. Enquiring about the

The arrest of Gavrilo Princip. The archduke's assassin was in danger of being lynched, and was already badly beaten by the time he was taken to the police station for questioning.

Franz Ferdinand's bloodstained jacket, now on display in the Museum of Military History, Vienna.

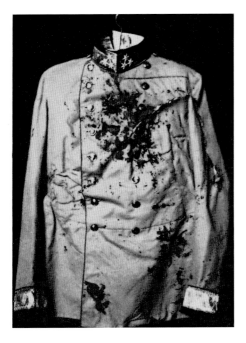

archduke's pain, Harrach was told, ever more faintly, 'It is nothing,' until the wounded man slipped into unconsciousness. Franz Ferdinand and the duchess were taken to the governor's residence; the latter was found to be dead on arrival, and the archduke died several minutes later.

Their assassin, Gavrilo Princip, attempted to turn the gun on himself but was apprehended by a furious crowd. It was only the arrival of the police that saved him from lynching. He swallowed cyanide, but it was not sufficient to kill him, and, bleeding and vomiting, he was taken to the police station. After a brief examination the police doctor declared Princip fit for trial. When proceedings commenced – on 12 October, four months after the assassination – details of the plot began to emerge. These pointed to a great upsurge in Serbian nationalist feeling, paralleling the rise of anarchist movements elsewhere in Europe and revealing terrorist techniques that had developed over the previous fifty years. Initially, however, what was perhaps most striking about Princip and his six principal co-conspirators was their youth: five of them, including Princip, were not yet twenty years old.[4] Could these young men, some little more than boys, really have planned the assassination themselves? And what had they been trying to achieve? The presiding judge, Leo Pfeffer, described them as:

> callow, hesitant, not grasping the seriousness of the judicial
> enquiry ... they involuntarily talked and disclosed things
> that were not asked of them. It is really a miracle that with

The conspirators on trial for the assassination in October 1914. The presiding judge was struck above all by their youth (only two of them were over twenty). In the front row are five of the seven principal collaborators: (from left to right) Trifko Grabež, Nedeljko Čabrinović, Gavrilo Princip, Danilo Ilić and Misko Jovanović.

young men still so raw and irresponsible nothing leaked out before hand of the preparations for the outrage. Each of them regarded himself as a hero, but not one of them had the courage to fire.[5]

Indeed, during the course of their trial Princip's collaborators confessed to their lack of nerve. Nineteen-year-old Trifko Grabež explained in a letter to his father that he was unable to throw the bomb for fear of killing innocent people in the crowd; seventeen-year-old Vaso Čubrilović claimed that he hadn't fired his gun out of concern for the duchess. Neither reaction is that of the nihilistic anarchist or the hardened criminal, so what had brought these apparently compassionate young men to the brink of committing murder? The answer was to be found in the nascent Serbian nationalist movement. All the participants had been motivated by a fiercely passionate belief in the creation of a pan-Serbian state, and they saw themselves as participants in forging a new future for the southern Slavs of the Austro-Hungarian Empire. At the time of his arrest, Nedeljko Čabrinović described himself as a

The seal of the Black Hand, the secret society otherwise known as 'Union or Death'. The society's manifesto openly called for the promotion of pan-Slavism through terrorism.

Serb hero; prior to the assassination he had posed for a photograph as though he were seeking immortality in a pantheon of national martyrs. During the trial, despite the purposely misleading statements and contradictory evidence of the defendants, a picture began to emerge of their involvement with the secret nationalist movement known as Union or Death, or, to its enemies, the Black Hand.

Like many movements of the 19th century, Serbian nationalism remained a political force in the 1910s and 1920s. South-Slavic self-determination was the primary goal for all Southern Slavs who felt outraged by the annexation of Bosnia and Herzegovina by Austria-Hungary in 1878. As in the 19th century, many of these nationalist ideas were promoted by the intelligentsia – students, journalists, teachers and young academics – who formed groups to promote Slavic unity. One such was the very popular Slavic South, founded in Belgrade in 1904. That year, the city hosted a conference of South-Slavic writers – the First Congress of Yugoslav Youth – and over the next few years cultural events, demonstrations, newspapers and journals were all organized to highlight the Slavic cause.

The Black Hand was different, however. Founded in 1911 by Colonel Dragutin Dimitrijević, among others, it grew out of the spirit of violent Balkan nationalism that had surfaced at the turn of the century. Most notable were the Comitaji: a group of armed Macedonian agitators who, with funding from the Bulgarian government, carried out a series of violent terrorist acts between 1902 and 1912 – destroying bridges, attacking police and committing murder – as an attempt to involve Europe in ending Ottoman rule in Macedonia. Serb revolutionary groups followed their lead, resulting in the foundation of the Serbian Comitaji in 1905. The aim of the Black Hand, according to its manifesto, was the unification of all Serbs through terrorism rather than political propaganda. Dimitrijević had firmly established his credentials by taking part in the brutal murder of the Serbian king and queen, Alexander and Drago, in 1903 – the result of a plot by a clique of military officers, many of whom would continue their involvement in violent nationalist movements after the coup.

The Black Hand owed its existence not just to the organized revolutionary nationalism on the rise in the Balkan states. It was also influenced by a tradition of secret societies that dated back to the 18th century. The violent and illegal nature of its activities demanded secrecy from its members, as was clearly laid down in the manifesto; but it was also the case that secret societies in general were popular among young working- and middle-class Serbs as a way of forging links between like-minded people. Unlike the older generation and the upper classes, the young were unwilling to put their trust in the ascent of the Archduke Franz Ferdinand (1863–1914) to the Habsburg throne, and doubted that it would improve the lot of the average Serb. Of course, part of the appeal of organizations such as the Black Hand would have been their clandestine nature. These groups were organized through networks of 'agents', who were known only by numbers or codenames, and linked through intermediaries to ensure that the total number of members was known to very few people. They had their roots in the secret fraternal societies of the 18th century – such as Freemasonry – that had been popular in France and England as places in which the philosophical ideas of the Enlightenment could be discussed. Originally intended as no more than social and intellectual clubs, during the French revolution they acquired a more sinister reputation. The often fluid exchange of membership between the radical Jacobin clubs and the Freemasons contributed to the belief that the French revolution was the result of a conspiracy plotted by secret societies. The idea that conspiracy was central, if not crucial, to bringing about social change became more widespread, and it was reinforced by Gracchus Babeuf's 'Conspiracy of Equals' plot, uncovered in 1796. Although he was not an anarchist per se, Babeuf's call for a popular armed uprising to overthrow the government is often considered a precursor to 19th-century anarchist theory. The plot was a failure (owing mainly to the garrulousness of its participants) and would have been forgotten as a minor incident during a particularly eventful period of history had

Freemasonry became associated with revolutionary political activity during the French revolution, when many members of the Jacobin clubs were also Freemasons (note the figure wearing the liberty cap on the left). This tradition of esoteric secret societies orchestrating conspiratorial plots persisted into the 19th century and continues even today.

Peter Kropotkin, a leading Russian anarchist whose writings inspired a wave of anarchist violence throughout Europe in the late 19th and early 20th centuries.

overleaf In 1881 the Russian nationalist group Narodnaya Volya ('The People's Will') killed Tsar Alexander II by throwing a bomb as he descended from his carriage in St Petersburg. The aim of fomenting terror was at the heart of the anarchist manifesto. The spot where the tsar was assassinated is now marked by the Church of Our Saviour on Spilled Blood.

it not been picked up in the 1820s by groups such as the Italian Carbonari and the Russian Decembrists. The idea that secrecy and conspiratorial behaviour could be used as a tactic to effect social and political change had taken root. But this was not the only influence acting on the young nationalists. Of equal importance were the ideas of certain 19th-century radicals, which were picked up, modified and employed in the service of emerging nationalist movements.

In the student cafés and taverns of Belgrade, political theories, particularly those of the Russian anarchists Peter Kropotkin and Mikhail Bakunin, were avidly discussed and debated. A founding father of anarchism, Peter Kropotkin was born into a noble family in 1842 and had become politically radicalized as a young man. Although he himself was an intellectual and a theorist, writing his most important works from his place of exile in London, his philosophy influenced anarchist action during the late 19th and early 20th centuries. As he wrote in his newspaper *Le Révolté*, this philosophy was based on 'Permanent revolt by word of mouth, in writing, by the dagger, the rifle, dynamite … Everything is good for us which falls outside legality.'[6] For the young Serbs hoping to bring about social change, terrorism as a form of direct action – what the anarchists described as 'propaganda of the deed' – seemed the most immediate way of focusing attention on their grievances and rallying the masses behind them. 'I have seen our people being steadily ruined, I am a peasant's son and I know what goes on in the

villages. This is why I meant to take my revenge and I regret nothing,'[7] said Princip at his trial. Although his aims were nationalist, Princip's statement is reminiscent of 19th-century anarchist views, most notably the quest to avenge social wrongs and a complete absence of remorse.

The character of the ruthless political radical was summed up by Bakunin in his description of the anarchist Sergei Nechaev as 'one of those fanatical young men who know no doubts, who fear nothing'.[8] The *Catechism of a Revolutionary*, written by Bakunin and Nechaev in 1869, reveals an enthusiastic advocacy of terrorism in the name of anarchism. It describes the fundamental creed of revolution as follows:

> *The Revolutionist is a doomed man. He has no private interests, no affairs, sentiments, ties, property, nor even a name of his own. His entire being is devoured by one purpose, one thought, one passion – the revolution. Heart and soul, not merely by word but by deed, he has severed every link with the social order and with the entire civilized world; with the laws, good manners, conventions, and morality of that world. He is its merciless enemy and continues to inhabit it with only one purpose – to destroy it.*[9]

Although Bakunin soon became disillusioned with Nechaev and broke all ties with him, their collaboration made overt the connection between social revolution and terrorist activity. His description of Nechaev provides almost a template for those who sought to join these groups – young men 'who have decided in an absolute way that many, very many of them, must perish at the hands of the government, but who will not stop because of that until the … people rise. They are magnificent, these young fanatics, believers without gods, heroes without phrases.'[10]

Despite high-profile incidents such as the assassination of Tsar Alexander II by the Russian nationalist group Narodnaya Volya (the 'People's Will'), much anarchist activity in Europe and the United States was really the work of individuals, few of whom were politicized to any significant degree, let alone involved in the sophisticated networks the authorities believed to exist. The basic tenets of anarchism – which, as Bakunin wrote, 'recognize no other activity but the work of extermination'[11] – allowed the misfit, the loner, the psychopath to mete out his revenge on a society he believed had forsaken him. Yet anarchist activity offered 19th-century radicals a new means of revolutionary political expression. Assassination was now one aspect of 'propaganda of the deed', and it is in this context that the assassination of Archduke Franz Ferdinand differs from the political murders of previous centuries.

Princip and his co-conspirators are a clear illustration of developments that took place in the later 19th century – not just in terms of ideology but in methodology, too. Although they were neither anarchists nor terrorists, but rather self-avowed nationalists, they borrowed the tactics of these other groups; in this they represent the new face of political murder that began to emerge at this time. Since antiquity, the murder of a political figure – usually a king – had been accompanied by debates about the rights and wrongs of tyrannicide, with the assassin pointing to the unjust behaviour of the ruler as his defence, but assassinations in the 19th century were motivated by different concerns. Franz Ferdinand was Princip's chosen target not for what he did, but for what he represented. As an individual, he was not personally responsible for the injustices Princip and his fellow nationalists saw around them; he did not issue the cruel edicts of a tyrant, and his removal would not bring about a radical change in regime. Franz Ferdinand was chosen, following the example of the Comitaji, as a means of drawing attention to his assassins' demands. By bringing about his death, Princip and the other participants in the conspiracy would force the world to take notice of their plight. The impersonality of their choice of victim was matched by the impersonality of the means of assassination (they had planned to use explosives as well as pistols). This choice of weapons, with the attendant risks – the use of explosives inevitably introduces the possibility that innocent bystanders might be killed – also illustrates changes in political assassination that began to take place.

Between 1881 and 1914, five successful assassination plots were carried out on European heads of state – Tsar Alexander II (killed 1881), President Sadi Carnot of France (1894), Prime Minister Cánovas del Castillo of Spain (1897), Empress Elizabeth of Austria (1898) and King Umberto I of Italy (1900) – while in 1901 President William McKinley was assassinated in the United States. Queen Victoria was the target of two abortive attempts, in 1872 and 1882. Even those assassinations not carried out by anarchists used the destructive methods advocated by anarchist theorists – a member of the Narodnaya Volya group, for example, killed Tsar Alexander II by throwing a bomb as he descended

from his carriage. The need to create chaos was at the heart of the anarchist manifesto, represented by the *Catechism*'s call for 'utter destruction'. Assassins incorporated indiscriminate violence as a means of bringing about change irrespective of their ideology (or lack of one). No longer was the assassin required to be close to his victim: the handgun and the use of dynamite removed the need for any personal contact at all. (Some assassins still chose it, however: President McKinley's assassin, Leon Czolgosz, was close enough to speak to the president and shot him under the pretext of offering to shake his hand.)

It was perhaps this very impersonality that encouraged a move from killing a specific head of state (i.e. a tyrant), to killing the individual who best represents it, to destroying its abstract symbols. For it was during the 19th century that activists first attacked state institutions such as banks and stock exchanges, before they turned their attention to more generic symbols of the bourgeois classes such as cafés, theatres and music halls. These violent and increasingly indiscriminate acts, usually the work of individuals claiming anarchist beliefs, employed new methods of destruction that would become familiar with the rise of terrorism in the 20th century.

Although anarchist activity was widespread across Europe, France experienced the highest levels. In addition to the assassination of President Carnot in Lyon, there were eleven attacks in the period 1882–94, motivated by anarchist principles and planned to cause maximum damage to specific symbols of the establishment. In 1882 a music hall in Lyon became a target specifically because of its middle-class clientele, whom an anarchist paper described as 'the fine flower of the bourgeoisie and of commerce', it was thus decided that 'the first act of the social revolution must be to destroy this den'.[12] Later attacks in Paris, on the Stock Exchange in 1886 and the Chamber of Deputies in 1893, followed a similar pattern. Chosen for their symbolic value, these places were attacked by what can only be described as fanatical misfits seeking vengeance on society by whatever means. In the first attempt, Charles Gallo, who had acquired his anarchist ideology while serving a prison sentence for forgery, threw a bottle of sulphuric acid from a gallery of the Stock Exchange down onto the brokers and clerks below. At his trial, he shouted 'Long live anarchism! Death to the bourgeois judiciary!' Auguste Vaillant received the death sentence for throwing a home-made bomb into the crowded Chamber of Deputies. His anarchist principles also seemed to stem from the poverty of his existence rather than from a political ideology. François Claudius Koenigstein, known as Ravachol, was so active that he gave his name to the French verb *ravacholiser*, 'to blow up'. He began his career with the cruel and senseless murders of two vulnerable, destitute old men, before moving on to bomb the Paris apartment buildings where high-court judges were residing. Most extreme of all were the actions of Émile Henry, who appalled even anarchists when he bombed the busy Café Terminus near the Gare Saint-Lazare in Paris: its clientele were mainly modest shopkeepers and working men, of whom twenty were wounded and one killed. His reply to the accusation that he had killed innocent people was: 'There are no innocents.'

Anthropometric record of François Claudius Koenigstein, the anarchist known as Ravachol, who was responsible for bomb attacks on members of the Paris judiciary in 1892. The archetype of the bomb-throwing anarchist, Ravachol became a kind of hero of revolt.

The sheer number of attacks, all attributed to the same ideology, led some to suspect an extensive degree of cooperation among the perpetrators. This suspicion grew stronger following a meeting in 1881 in London of key European anarchist figures, which aimed to reconcile anarchist theory with the practice of 'propaganda of the deed'. This meeting seemed to confirm society's worst fears: that a vast and intricate web of anarchist cells existed across Europe. In reality, the group never met again, but it was enough to suggest a sophisticated level of organization. Anarchist literature seemed to confirm that there

'A Bomb at the Café Terminus', an illustration printed in the French Le Petit Journal, 26 February 1894. Émile Henry's bombing of this café near the Gare Saint-Lazare in Paris was seen as extreme even by anarchists: his victims were ordinary working men and women.

UNE BOMBE AU CAFE TERMINUS
Arrestation de l'assassin

was a ruthlessly efficient anarchist conspiracy to destroy the world, and the blame for direct action seemed to lead back to the anarchist philosopher in his library. The figure of the anarchist began to appear in contemporary fiction (Joseph Conrad's *The Secret Agent* and Henry James's *Princess Casamassima* are celebrated examples), either as a shadowy agent of destruction, sloping off into the night, or as a young idealist chafing against social injustice. Such portrayals contributed to the development of a cultural archetype, so that the anarchist became a bogeyman, easily recognizable in political cartoons, plays and other media. These popular incarnations were not mere entertainment, however, since they had a serious effect on political radicalism. On a popular level, they established and reinforced a link between terrorist–anarchist activity and

Franz Ferdinand and Sophie Chotek on the tennis court at Pressburg before their relationship was made public. Sophie had been a lady-in-waiting to the Archduchess Isabella of Pressburg, and was allowed to marry the archduke only on the understanding that their children would never succeed to the Habsburg throne.

political protest in general. In the United States, fears of the European anarchist were particularly potent, contributing to a persistent mistrust of foreigners as waves of different immigrant groups entered the country. This anxiety led to the miscarriage of justice that followed the Chicago Haymarket bombing in 1886, in which eight anarchist writers and agitators were found guilty of causing the death of a policemen. The ruling was based on evidence so slender as to be practically non-existent, but four of the accused were executed.

The conspirators who plotted to assassinate Archduke Franz Ferdinand can thus be seen as part of a Europe-wide wave of violent political action that had begun with the French revolution and gathered momentum in the 19th century, leading to the methods and tactics favoured by anarchists. (It should be noted that, although they advocated terrorism in theory, all except Princip and Čabrinović were unable to carry out what was expected of them. At their trial they admitted that they were unable to throw bombs at the archduke's car out of concern for the surrounding crowds.) In addition to the ethos of 'propaganda of the deed' was the allure of the secret society and the tradition of conspiracy to overthrow a government, all of which contributed to Princip's choice of assassination as a means of drawing attention to his nationalist ideology. How was it, then, that unlike equivalent crimes being performed across Europe, this act had repercussions that resounded across the world?

Franz Ferdinand, nephew of Emperor Franz Joseph, had become heir to the Austro-Hungarian Empire following the suicide of Franz Joseph's son, Archduke Rudolf. A sickly, consumptive man, Franz Ferdinand was not expected to live long enough to reign, but he recovered his health sufficiently to make a contentious choice of bride: Countess Sophie Chotek, a lady-in-waiting to the Archduchess Isabella. Countess Sophie's family, although aristocratic, was penniless and of insufficient rank, meaning that she was considered an unsuitable spouse for the heir to the Habsburg throne. Franz Ferdinand refused to back down, and a morganatic marriage was finally agreed. Fourteen years to the day before his assassination, he signed a deed renouncing his children's right to inherit the throne. This apparent strength of character had an ugly side, however: Franz Ferdinand was hot-headed and violent, enjoying nothing more than letting off round after round of gunshot during hunting parties, to the terror of onlookers. Relations with the ageing emperor were difficult, characterized by a mutual fear and distrust. The archduke was also a bully and was the cause of frequent ugly scenes at court, crying out when crossed: 'When I am commander-in-chief I shall do as I will; if anyone does anything else I shall have them shot.'[13] His irascible behaviour led to rumours that he was clinically insane and should be prevented from inheriting.

Austria-Hungary was second only to the Russian Empire in size; stretching across Central Europe, it comprised eleven different

The bodies of Franz Ferdinand and Sophie lying in state in Vienna. Even in death, Sophie's lower rank caused diplomatic problems. Were it not for the intervention of Emperor Franz Joseph, she would not have been allowed to lie next to a Habsburg. Nonetheless, her coffin was noticeably lower and less ornate than her husband's.

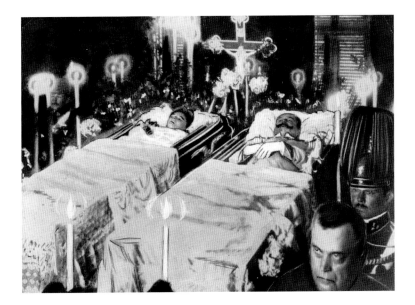

nationalities, fourteen recognized languages (as well as many that were not recognized) and fifty million people. It had succeeded the Austrian Empire, having been established in 1867 as a compromise between the Habsburg dynasty, which had ruled parts of Europe since the 13th century, and the Magyar nobility of Hungary. The empire's dualist structure meant that Hungary had its own parliament in Budapest even if it recognized the Austrian Emperor Franz Joseph as king of Hungary. But this arrangement did not allow for, nor recognize, the differing histories and conflicting demands of the empire's diverse ethnicities: in its very diversity lay the origins of discord. Most of Austria-Hungary's 23 million Slavs had not supported the compromise, and it was their growing dissatisfaction that led to the emergence of Slavic nationalism.

Franz Ferdinand's visit to Sarajevo was arranged for 28 June – the feast day of St Vitus, the patron saint of Serbia, and the 525th anniversary of the Serbian defeat by Ottoman Turks in Kosovo. For over five hundred years it had been a national day of mourning, but for the first time in history, following a Serbian victory at Kumanovo in 1912, it was to be celebrated. It was not, therefore, a particularly auspicious day for a visit by the heir to the Habsburg throne. Indeed, the archduke had premonitions prior to the journey and even discussed postponing it, although this may have been due to his own idiosyncrasies rather than any sensitivity to Serb feeling. He was known to be superstitious, and enjoyed recounting the prediction of a fortune-teller who advised him that 'he would one day let loose a world war'.[14] On the day of his departure from Vienna, the electricity in his train carriage malfunctioned and the interior was lit by candles instead. Clearly not one to miss an opportunity for melodrama, the archduke was heard to comment that the lighting was 'like in a tomb'. He had reason to be apprehensive: the warm welcome in the press could not disguise the disaffection, increasing over the past two years, felt by the southern Slavs towards the Habsburg monarchy.

Princip and the other conspirators gave conflicting evidence during their trial, whether through bravado, an attempt to protect others in the plot, or genuine ignorance of the conspiracy's extent. When he was first arrested, Princip refused to name names, insisting that the assassination was his idea alone. Čabrinović was apprehended the following day; his confession – more freely given than Princip's – shed light on the Comitaji's involvement, which had provided the group with bombs and money. The blanket arrest of all young Serbs known to have some connection with the two suspects led the police to the remaining Appel Quay accomplices, who would stand trial

A soldier kneels at the graveside of a fallen companion in a huge cemetery dedicated to Serbs killed during an Austrian bombardment in 1915. Franz Ferdinand's assassination is viewed as the harbinger of a new – and more violent – order.

alongside Princip and Čabrinović in October. Interrogations during July continued to unearth participants who had provided funding, weapons or safe houses. In the end, a total of twenty-five stood trial for the assassination of the archduke. Of those who were on the Appel Quay at the time of the first, abortive bomb, five were too young to receive the death penalty, and were instead sentenced to between thirteen and twenty years' imprisonment. Princip and Čabrinović both served only a few years before dying in prison of tuberculosis.

The Austro-Hungarian government was convinced that Serbian local government had been involved in the plot and responded severely, determined to stamp out any evidence of nationalism. On 23 July 1914 it issued an ultimatum requiring that the assassins be brought to justice. Its harsh terms and its demands for deference from Serbia prompted the British foreign secretary, Edward Grey, to comment that he had 'never before seen one State address to another independent State a document of so formidable a character'. As was expected, Serbia rejected the ultimatum, and Austria-Hungary had the excuse it needed to declare war on Serbia, which it did on 28 July 1914. The chain of events that would lead to World War I had been set in motion.

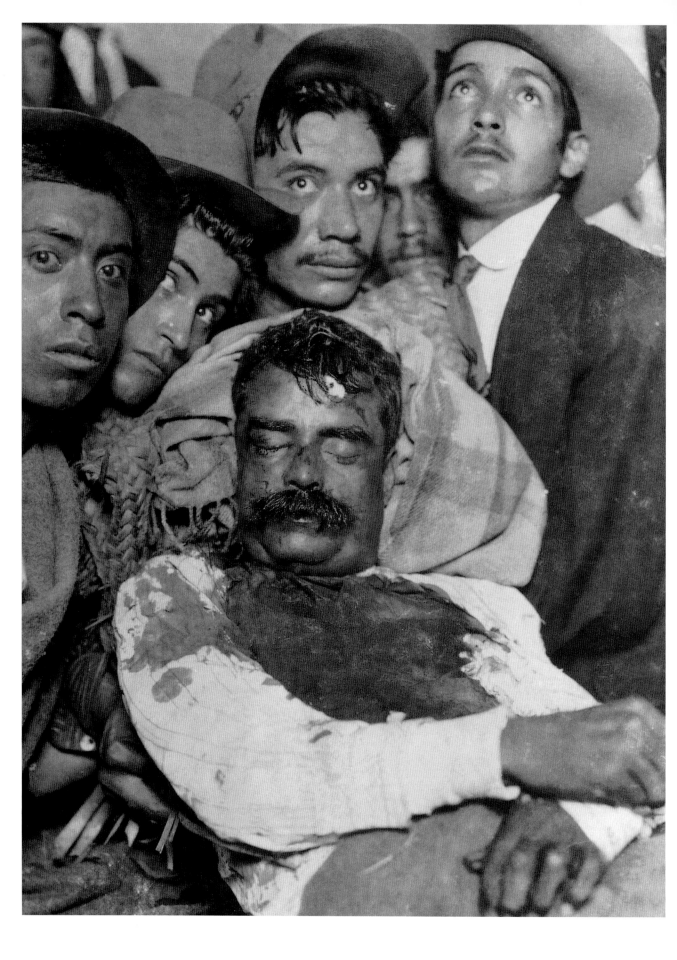

chapter 6

From Outlaws to Icons:
Emiliano Zapata and Pancho Villa

There is no doubt that history is written by the victors. But it is also true
that legends are written by the people.[1]

Early 20th-century Mexico was a vast, fragmented country. The north
was an often arid land of extensive cattle estates, commercial agriculture
and large mining enterprises, inhabited by a highly mobile population.
The south, however, had a large indigenous population settled in
traditional villages, some still independent but many absorbed within
large estates. Spanish rule, which had ended in 1821, had bequeathed
a hierarchy based on ethnicity; and although the country's president,
Porfirio Díaz, had native ancestry, evidence of indigenous descent
became noticeably scarcer the higher one went up the socio-economic
scale. The hacienda system – in which the majority of the country's
land was owned by a select few but worked by the local population –
had dominated much of the countryside for over three hundred years
and had expanded in the last decades of the 19th century. In the state
of Morelos in the south – the birthplace of Emiliano Zapata – over half
of the surface area was owned by a mere thirty haciendas, while the
indigenous population lived in grinding poverty, uneducated and often
permanently indebted to the local landowners. The political regime was
limited by nepotism and corruption, which restricted access to business
and political opportunities to a favoured few. The lower classes were
kept in order by brutal methods, and the middle class was excluded from
office and repressed if it became too ambitious.

Thirty-four of Mexico's hundred years as an independent country
had been under the rule of Díaz, who had ensured his political longevity
by governing the country with a policy he described as 'pan o palo'
('bread or the club'). He installed yes-men to rule as governors in distant
provinces, knowing that they would feel loyal to his regime rather than
to the people they were meant to represent; he rigged elections to
Congress and the Supreme Court; and he struck deals with landowners
and other members of the elite that were to the detriment of the majority.
Those who could not be won over by the promise of deals or money
were threatened or murdered. Stringent laws relating to 'unpatriotic' or

The body of Emiliano Zapata after his
shooting at Chinameca. So powerful was
the legend surrounding him that, despite
public viewings of his corpse, many of
his countrymen refused to believe he was
dead, convinced that a double had been
ambushed in his place.

Porfirio Díaz, president of Mexico between 1876–1880 and 1884–1911. Forced from office at the onset of the revolution, Díaz fled to Paris, where he died four years later.

'seditious' opinions meant that journalists critical of the regime could be imprisoned without trial and their newspapers shut down. Diaz's cronies and informers were present at all levels of government, enabling him to maintain control of his huge country and, with relative ease, to quash into submission any rebellions or attempts at opposition. The result was a regime that set the elite against the ambitious middle class, the landowner against the village, and those of Spanish descent against the indigenous population. As the president approached his eightieth birthday, in September 1910, it seemed that nothing could stop it.

The great event was marked by a series of costly and elaborate spectacles for hundreds of international dignitaries. Over several days, guests of the president enjoyed lavish dinners and spectacular firework displays in the capital, seeing nothing of the real country and little of the real Mexico City, whose unsanitary slums were home to a large underclass. But Díaz was only concealing from his visitors what he had ignored for so long. The regime had become complacent and, when revolution ignited in 1910, he and his whole bloated administration were caught off-guard. It was the unlikely figure of Francisco Madero – a wealthy landowner, physically slight, teetotal and vegetarian – who called for the overthrow of the Díaz government, and the entire nation rose to the challenge. The idea that the country was, or even could be, united in its aims was, however, illusory. The ensuing revolution was more the result of a timely coming together of grievances than a shared ideology. Madero's movement appealed to an educated, urban elite, and ignored the concerns of both the rural poor and the industrialized working class, both of which, in any event, had their own specific concerns. Nonetheless, despite Mexico's size and its different ethnicities, identities and cultures, there were simultaneous outbreaks of dissent in north and south. Landless peasants were motivated by land reform, workers formed unions – many of them founded by anarchists – and a confident middle class of minor landowners, schoolteachers and small-time lawyers made a grab for political power. The result was the successful overthrow of a seemingly invincible regime.

The next decade was turbulent for Mexico, which experienced a period of great upheaval and internecine fighting after Diaz's formal resignation in 1911. Madero's presidency was short-lived: he was assassinated during the 'Ten Tragic Days' of February 1913, to be replaced by General Victoriano Huerta, who himself was forced out a year later by Venustiano Carranza. During this period each of Mexico's leaders encountered, briefly cooperated with and then clashed bloodily with the revolutionary figures Emiliano Zapata and Francisco 'Pancho'

Venustiano Carranza addresses a crowd in the city of Saltillo. He established a provisional government in 1914, but relations with Zapata and Villa had been tense from the start, and in September 1914 they broke off all formal contact.

Villa, whose deeds made them legends in their own lifetime and whose legacies live on in Mexico today.

North and south, so vastly different in topography, culture and ethnicity, each produced their own folk hero. These men came to represent much more than their initial political causes, their larger-than-life personas eventually standing for the nation itself. The lives of Emiliano Zapata and Pancho Villa were endlessly told and retold in ballads, stories and films, fine-tuned and polished to become an inextricable part of Mexico's identity. In the decades that followed their deaths, successive governments co-opted their reputations as proof of their own commitment to Mexico and its values, using the memory of the revolution's heroes in a bid to prove the integrity of their own regimes. To this end, the authorities had to reconfigure the meaning of Villa and Zapata's rebellion, and by extension the meaning of the revolution itself. This also meant underplaying or sidestepping the stories of their violent deaths at the hands of the existing government.

Emiliano Zapata (1879–1919) came from the rural south, from the fertile, sugar-cane producing region of Morelos, agriculturally one of the

country's richest. He was a *mestizo* – of mixed native and European ancestry – an ethnic group that, at the time of the revolution, made up half of Mexico's population. Although the legend of his life quickly overtook reality, his family was not, as myth would have it, the poorest of the poor; they owned some livestock and a little land. In an area dominated by the powerful hacienda system, owning land meant that they were better off than many of their neighbours. Since the 1870s, as the sugar-cane industry grew in importance, plots of communal village land – including an orchard once belonging to Zapata's family – had been appropriated by larger and more powerful landowners. Part of the Zapata legend, endlessly repeated in newspapers after his death, tells the story of how he was struck by the injustice of this system, even as a child; how he swore to his father, 'When I am a man, I will make them give back our land.' Whether or not Zapata experienced the same levels of deprivation as his countrymen, his was not an easy life. He had at least a rudimentary education and was trained in bookkeeping, but when he rose to prominence as a revolutionary leader the urban elite and the press mocked him as barely literate (this in a country where only fifteen per cent of the population could read). His followers were likewise characterized as little more than a subhuman rabble. This stereotype of the savage peasant revolutionary, like all such stereotypes, was a convenient way to demonize Zapata and his followers, and allowed the authorities to discredit his calls for land reform.

Zapata was a popular, sociable figure in his home village and admired for his outstanding horsemanship. He had always taken pride in the way he looked, and the fitted, silver-buttoned trousers, wide hat and extravagant moustache that would make him instantly recognizable the world over were in evidence from early on. His striking appearance belied a diffident character, and he was, perhaps surprisingly, reserved in social situations, quietly spoken and almost shy. His fondness for women (he had perhaps as many as five illegitimate children) and gaming – particularly cock-fighting – all contributed to the image of a larger-than-life character.

In 1909, having been elected head of his village and tired of waiting for cumbersome bureaucratic machinery to return expropriated land to its original owners, Zapata galvanized eighty armed villagers into taking over land belonging to the local hacienda and farming it as their own. It was this that brought him wider attention, earning him the title of 'Attila of the South'. For Zapata and his followers, the reform of land ownership in the south was crucial for the liberation of the Mexican peasant, and throughout his life it remained his principal goal.

Emiliano Zapata in December 1913, six years before his death, as leader of the Liberation Army of the South.

President Victoriano Huerta and his cabinet. Huerta persecuted Zapata's followers with great vigour, and many were summarily executed. Having held onto power for one year, Huerta resigned the presidency on 15 July 1914, following repeated defeats at the hands of Obregón's and Villa's armies.

Zapata formalized this vision in his 'Plan de Ayala', which made its first appearance in 1911 but would be reissued three years later. Addressed 'to the Mexican People', it demanded the abolishment of the hacienda system and the complete restructuring of land ownership, as well as calling for universal suffrage and education.

When Madero took over the presidency in 1911, Zapata and his followers initially joined his cause but quickly became disillusioned when they realized that this new government was never going to do enough on the issue of land reform. This pattern – an early attempt at cooperation followed by animosity – would become characteristic of Zapata's dealings with each successive government. As Madero further humiliated Zapata by refusing him the governorship of Morelos, he and his followers took matters into their own hands, and bloody clashes between federal officers and Zapatistas led to lurid stories of machete-wielding bandits attacking white landowners. When Madero was assassinated in February 1913 and replaced by Huerta, the clashes between the Zapatistas and the government continued. In an attempt to secure their demands, Zapatistas patrolled the borders of Morelos, occupied towns and blew up trains. As the violence escalated, the press mesmerized its middle-class readership with tales of the barbarity of Zapata and his men, who were alleged to carry out surreally intricate forms of torture on their victims. Official reprisals were harsh: Huerta and his successors refused to deal with the Zapatistas, whom they considered terrorists, and many were summarily executed. A warrant for the arrest of Zapata made him an

*Irregular troops holding a position.
Uniformed soldiers were in a minority
during the revolution.*

outlaw. In a bid to raise funds to continue the struggle, Zapata devised
the idea of forcing hacienda owners to either pay a 'tax' or have their
fields burned to the ground. As a moneymaking scheme it was hugely
successful, but as a public relations effort considerably less so: reports
of fiendish, peyote-crazed Zapatistas featured ever more prominently
in the papers, terrifying the denizens of nearby Mexico City.

At the height of his influence, Zapata had command of over nearly
one third of the country and more than 20,000 followers. It was they
who marched into Mexico City in November 1914 to oust Venustiano
Carranza, who had established a provisional government and declared
himself president following Victoriano Huerta's resignation in July that
year. To the astonishment of onlookers, they were not the drug-fuelled
bandits of the popular press, but simple country folk, somewhat in awe
of the city's European luxuries and modern technology, who politely
removed their hats when requesting food or accommodation. Zapata
himself, rather than commandeering the most luxurious rooms the city
had to offer, stayed in a simple pension. The appearance of his army
initially invited derision: this was no well-oiled machine, but a motley
collection of men (and some women) wearing the traditional white
shirt and trousers of the southern peasant and riding a sorry assortment
of bony, bedraggled horses. Yet Zapata inspired such loyalty in his
followers that their lack of training and mismatched equipment did
nothing to dampen their revolutionary fervour: 'they rode in as heroes
and conquerors', said a foreign witness of Zapata's army.[2]

*overleaf Emiliano Zapata (centre,
in embroidered jacket) and Pancho Villa
(right, in uniform) ride into Mexico
City in December 1914.*

It was at this time that the historic meeting between Emiliano Zapata and his northern counterpart – Pancho Villa, known as the 'Centaur of the North' – took place just outside Mexico City in Xochimilco, on 4 December. Even though the two men later played similar roles in Mexican popular culture – the hero-bandit fighting for the rights of the little man – in reality there was a vast, and at first seemingly unbreachable, cultural gulf between them. Zapata looked comically incongruous in his wide-brimmed hat and silver-buttoned trousers; the khaki-clad Villa, in comparison, looked every inch the commander of the professional army he was. The impression given out by Zapata's country-bumpkin appearance was exacerbated by his taciturn demeanour and initial refusal to speak in anything but monosyllables. The two eyed one another without speaking for half an hour or so until, as they began to criticize Carranza and his followers, the ice was broken, each seeking to outdo the other with the creativity of his insults. As relations warmed, Zapata made his agenda clear. He was interested in pursuing the Plan de Ayala, to the exclusion of just about everything else – the larger issues of the country never concerned him. Villa agreed to the plan in principle without committing to anything concrete. They were united, however, in the fight against Carranza, and to this end Villa sent 35,000 of his men from the División del Norte to join the Zapatistas in Mexico City.

A few days later a photo was taken that would be shown around the world. As their armies joined in triumph in Mexico City, the two leaders entered the presidential palace. Seeing the ornately carved presidential chair, Villa sat in it and then, joking, repeatedly offered it to Zapata, who scowled and refused it: 'I didn't fight for that. I fought to get the lands back. I don't care about politics. We should burn the chair to end all ambitions.'[3] The photo of an expansive Villa at ease in the throne next to a baleful-looking Zapata convinced the rest of the world that Villa was the new leader of Mexico. In fact, neither was interested in the presidency for himself, wanting simply to fight the current government – a fact that more than one historian has pointed to as the reason for the revolution's ultimate failure. It seems that, having successfully occupied Mexico City, they were not sure what to do with it. They would never meet again: while Villa stayed on in the capital, enjoying its worldly distractions, Zapata returned to his beloved Morelos, as ever concerned only with the return of lands to the people.

When Carranza was officially elected president in 1917, he categorically rejected Zapata's Plan de Ayala; as so often before, Zapata and his followers found themselves at loggerheads with the government. After years of vicious guerrilla warfare, Zapata succeeded in driving

VILLA EN LA SILLA PRESIDENCIAL.

Villa and Zapata in the National Palace, 6 December 1914. The sight of Villa sitting in the presidential chair convinced the world that he was to be Mexico's next president.

Carranza's army from Morelos. However, victory was hollow: Carranza still ruled the rest of the country, and Morelos had been devastated by the fighting, its countryside ravaged and its people traumatized and starving. Although Zapata's demands for agrarian reform were still rejected, Carranza could not take the region as long as Zapata enjoyed the loyalty of his people. No matter how they suffered physically or materially, their faith in Zapata was unshakeable. The government could only recapture Morelos by removing Zapata.

On 9 April 1919, Zapata was lured into a trap. A Carrancista officer, Jesús Guajardo, was promising to defect; Zapata considered him be one of the most skilled cavalry officers in the federal army, and he would have been a valuable prize. Despite warnings that the arrangement was a federal plot, Zapata agreed to meet Guajardo in person on the understanding that both would bring only thirty men. As Zapata's entourage headed towards the agreed meeting place, great clouds of dust could be seen in the distance, thrown up by the 600 federal troops accompanying Guajardo. Despite this, Zapata welcomed him and even rode with him into the countryside, agreeing to see him again the next day at a hacienda in Chinameca, in the Ayala municipality of Morelos. The following afternoon Zapata, having placed sentries outside, entered the hacienda's courtyard with only ten men. He was met by Guajardo's ranked troops. A bugler played three long notes – as if to honour the guest – and as the third died away the soldiers raised their guns and fired at Zapata, two at point-blank range. The firing continued; five of Zapata's men were killed and four wounded, while those remaining fled south.

Zapata's bullet-ridden corpse was a bounty too valuable to hide away. Guajardo ordered it to be carried by mule to Cuautla, approximately 15 miles (24 km) away, where news of the ambush had been wired in advance. As the procession reached the town's central square, Zapata's body was cut from the mule and allowed to tumble into the dust; from there it was dragged to the police station and formally identified. Photographs of the body and of the burial two days later were shown around the world. Despite this, rumours circulated – particularly among his Morelos countrymen – that Zapata was not dead. Among them was a theory suggesting that Zapata had sent a decoy in his place to meet Guajardo, and that the real Emiliano Zapata was living up in the mountains: some claimed to have glimpsed a distant figure on horseback, still fighting for the *Tierra y Libertad* – 'Land and Liberty' – of his countrymen. For his role in the plot, Guajardo was made a general and received over 5,000 pesos.

Questions remain about Zapata's uncharacteristically reckless behaviour leading up to the assassination. Given the suspicious behaviour of Guajardo and the federal troops, why had Zapata followed through with the meeting at the hacienda? One story perseveres: that Zapata had been warned of his death by a *curandera* or folk healer, and that he had met his fate willingly, sacrificing himself to the cause of revolutionary Mexico. He was known to have discussed historical figures glorified by death and political movements strengthened by the assassination of their leaders, almost as if he acknowledged that violent death was the only suitable ending for a life such as his. In reality, Zapata's unusual lack of caution was probably due to his desperate need for arms and for more men, but as his memory becomes ever more confused with myth the idea of self-martyrdom persists.

Although his motives were different, Francisco 'Pancho' Villa (1878–1923) came to occupy a similar place in folklore. He was from Chihuahua in the north, a land dominated by vast plains and the mountains of the Sierra Madre whose economy was based on mines and haciendas. He was born Doroteo Arango, into an extremely poor family about whom little is known. At the age of seventeen he was alleged to have murdered a local landowner's son for raping his sister, after which

Pancho Villa on horseback, accompanied by troops from his División del Norte, outside the northern town of Ojinaga, 1916.

Pancho Villa posing with his most trusted men – the Dorados ('Golden Ones'), whose marksmanship, even on horseback, was legendary.

he went into hiding in the hills and lived among bandits. This story carries all the seeds of the Villa myth: the outlaw righting a wrong through violence, fighting authority on behalf of the oppressed, and managing to elude capture. From these few scraps of information Villa evolved into a character that would be known around the world as the embodiment of the Mexican revolution.

When the first rumblings of revolution sounded across the country, Villa was quick to join the Maderistas. He already had a certain notoriety among landowners, and some celebrity among the *campesinos* (peasant farmers), as a cattle thief, and he quickly rose to become one of Madero's generals. His local origins, intimate knowledge of the region and reputation for toughness soon earned him the respect of his men. Already, reports of his staggering cruelty alternated with accounts of his lavish sentimentality: he was known to have granted one enemy reprieve because he was moved by the man's tears. This dichotomy would characterize stories about Pancho Villa throughout his lifetime and beyond. The press liked to describe him in terms that were non-human: he was a troglodyte, a jaguar, the 'Centaur of the North'; a force of nature, as unstoppable as a hurricane or an earthquake. Such tales contributed to the idea that Villa had won a following through sheer charisma, and it was said that he could rouse his dejected, exhausted troops simply by appearing on horseback among them.

Unlike Zapata, whose proximity to Mexico City meant that the literate classes perceived him as a real threat, Villa was sufficiently distant to be a somewhat thrilling figure, even to those who were his sworn enemies. The allure of the bandit–revolutionary, avoiding all capture and outwitting the authorities, soon spread to the United States, where Villa's exploits featured regularly in the tabloid press. During the volatile decade of 1910–20 reputations and fortunes were made and lost with bewildering speed, and Villa's was no exception. When Madero came to power in 1911, Villa was at the vanguard of the people's movement. A respected general leading an army of 35,000 troops, he represented the popular uprising, a renegade hero who came from the same stock as his followers and understood their plight and their dreams. But in 1915, with Carranza in power, this all changed. The new government's conscious attempt to win over the masses had rendered Villa superfluous. The country no longer needed him as a symbol of its revolutionary dreams, since the government seemed set to fulfil them. In a mere three years, the former general had become marginalized, living in the mountains of Chihuahua with a handful of trusted retainers.

At this point Villa's reputation in the United States also underwent a seismic shift. Up till now he had been seen as the popular face of democratic principles – in many ways an incarnation of that beloved American figure, the vigilante frontiersman confronting the greedy corruption of the Old World. His exploits thrilled the masses, and he even appeared in several American films, including the 1914 *Life of General Villa*. This benevolent fascination came to an abrupt end in the autumn of 1915, when President Woodrow Wilson's administration recognized Carranza's government, an act that completely turned Villa against his powerful neighbour to the north: 'From this moment on, I will devote my life to the killing of every gringo I can get my hands on and to the destruction of all gringo property.'[4] He was true to his word, and he and 500 men carried out an attack on the garrison town of Columbus, New Mexico, on 9 March 1916. Information Villa had received prior to the attack led him to believe that only 50 troops were stationed in the town; in fact, there were more like 600 and, as the day drew to a close, 17 Americans and over 100 Villistas lay dead. Reasons for the raid are still not clear, but it intensified Villa's reputation on both sides of the border, making him Public Enemy Number One in the United States and restoring his popularity at home.

PROCLAMATION
$5,000⁰⁰ REWARD

FRANCISCO (PANCHO) VILLA

ALSO $1,000. REWARD FOR ARREST OF
CANDELARIO CERVANTES, PABLO LOPEZ,
FRANCISCO BELTRAN, MARTIN LOPEZ

ANY INFORMATION LEADING TO HIS APPREHENSION WILL
BE REWARDED.

CHIEF OF POLICE
Columbus
New Mexico

MARCH 9, 1916

An American poster offering a reward for the arrest of Pancho Villa after his attack on Columbus, New Mexico, on 9 March 1916.

Villa's attack on American soil occurred as Wilson was facing re-election; the president was obliged not only to act, but also to be seen to act decisively. A week after the raid on Columbus, General John Pershing's punitive expedition was launched, in which 4,800 soldiers (later increased to 10,000) marched into Mexico in pursuit of Villa. It was both a public relations and a military fiasco. Even those Mexicans who had been horrified by the attack on their powerful neighbour were overcome with patriotic fervour once the United States army was in their country. President Carranza was initially cooperative but soon withdrew his support, refusing to aid the expedition. United States troops suffered terribly in the extremes of the Mexican climate, swooning in stultifying heat by day and freezing by night. They were at a huge disadvantage, marching through inhospitable and unfamiliar terrain, and were dependent on the goodwill of locals, who met them with, at best, silent resentment and, at worst, open hostility. They were no match for Villa and his men, who knew the surrounding hills intimately and had the support of their people. While on the run from Pershing and his troops, Villa sustained a serious knee injury and was obliged to hide for months in a cave up a mountainside while he regained his strength. On one occasion, lying at the mouth of the cave, he saw Pershing's men pass just a few hundred feet below him, yet he was not captured. By 5 February 1917 the exhausted troops withdrew, having succeeded only in bringing the United States to the brink of war with Mexico. For Villa, it was an unmitigated success, with America's humiliating defeat cementing his role as a national hero. As news of his exploits spread, it confirmed him as the epitome of the cunning outlaw, outwitting the cumbersome might of the American military machine. Episodes from the abortive expedition soon entered national mythology and became the stuff of popular ballads, still played well into the 1950s. Villa had gone from revolutionary hero to has-been and back again, but his position in Mexican legend was now assured.

Villa may have been beloved by the people, but his rehabilitation did not extend to the Mexican government, who still considered him an outlaw. However, with advancing years Villa appeared to be mellowing, and by 1920 he had managed to negotiate a government pension, a hacienda and funds for the upkeep of fifty armed bodyguards. Some saw this as evidence that Villa had been paid off, while others criticized the government for funding criminals. The press, meanwhile, depicted Villa as the retired general living out his final days in tranquillity.

The reality, of course, was less straightforward. Retirement did not come easily: Villa trusted no one, was constantly vigilant, and was constantly haunted by fears of assassination. He was rarely without his

fifty handpicked bodyguards, was known to be uncomfortable about people walking behind him and never slept in the same place twice. Nonetheless, Villa's reputation for brutality had given way to one for fatherly concern. He built a school for 300 local children on his hacienda; he received literally hundreds of requests to be a godfather, a role that he took seriously; and he had several children of his own, by different women. On the morning of 10 July 1923, he set off to attend a christening in the village of Río Florida, about 50 miles (80 km) from his home, where he was going to act as godfather to a friend's child. He dismissed recent rumours that his life was in danger, even travelling without his usual number of escorts. As he drove through the village of Parral, he was unaware of how close he had come to death: as he approached a busy junction, several rifles were pointed at him from the windows of adjacent buildings. He was saved by the arrival of hundreds of schoolchildren swarming into the intersection from a nearby school.

Ten days later, on the return journey, he was not so lucky. At the same junction, Villa's car was met with a rousing 'Viva Villa!', the old cry from his days as general of the División del Norte. Rather than a tribute, however, this heralded his death, being the signal for gunmen in a nearby apartment to open fire. The car was hit by forty bullets, nine of which hit Villa, killing him instantly. His chauffeur and one of his assistants were also killed at the scene, and the three remaining passengers, Villa's escorts, were wounded, two fatally. Once they were certain Villa was dead, his assassins slowly rode out of town, seemingly confident that they would be neither pursued nor arrested. Suspicions that the murder had been an official rather than a personal affair were heightened by the fact that the telegraph service was suspended immediately after his death, preventing news from reaching his estate for six hours.

Villa's funeral in Parral, on 21 July 1923, was carried out with great ceremony. Thousands of mourners followed the coffin to the cemetery,

Jesús Salas Barraza confessed to the murder of Pancho Villa, claiming sole responsibility. He was sentenced to twenty years in prison, but was released after only three months. No one else was ever investigated.

where Villa was buried with the honours appropriate to a former general in the military. As news of his death spread round the world, newspaper reports of his life ranged from the critical to the laudatory. Many maintained the idea of Villa as a force of nature, an uneducated 'diamond in the rough', reinforcing the myth that persists today. Within Mexico, the reaction was similar: depending on the political affiliation of the newspaper, Villa was either hailed as a hero or vilified as a murderer, a thief and worse. Questions remained unanswered about the identity of Villa's killers, and suspicion fell on President Obregón's administration. Although it denied any involvement, the casual exit of the killers and the failure of the telegraph service – not to mention the absence of any troops in Parral, a garrison town, on the day of the murder – led many to believe that the government was involved in, or at least aware of, the plot. Two weeks after the funeral, the government had still not been seen to take any action to identify the killers. Suspicions continued to mount until a local politician, Jesús Salas Barraza, confessed to sole responsibility for the murder. Fears that this seemed a convenient, face-saving turn of events for the Mexican government were confirmed when Barraza was later pardoned and released after serving only three months of his twenty-year sentence.

In death, the two revolutionary figures played similar roles in the Mexican imagination. As the events of the revolution receded into the past and the period took on the gloss of myth, Emiliano Zapata and Pancho Villa began to represent very different characteristics from those they had exhibited in life. And although the manner of their deaths was partly responsible for creating this mythology – Zapata was correct in recognizing that nothing enhances a reputation like perceived martyrdom – successive Mexican governments also contributed to their evolving legends and exploited them as a means of defining their own ideologies.

The rehabilitation of Zapata began slowly. The first anniversary of his death was barely acknowledged, except at a local level, but over the years it was commemorated with increasing ceremony, not just in Morelos but in the whole of Mexico. For both figures, those character traits that in their lifetimes had earned them the reprobation of the conservative press became whitewashed. Their lack of education was now presented as peasant integrity, their brutality was now seen as courage in the face of the bourgeois oppressor, and their often cruel treatment of women and their fathering of numerous illegitimate children were signs of virility. Zapata in particular was increasingly portrayed as a romantic hero. School textbooks played down the

The scene of Villa's assassination in Parral, Chihuahua, on 20 July 1923; the revolutionary leader is slumped in his seat, behind the body of his chauffeur. The car was hit by forty bullets, nine of which hit Villa, killing him instantly.

A coin from Villa's pocket, perforated during the attack.

ignominious details of his death and the government's role in it, emphasizing instead his personal strengths and equating them with positive aspects of Mexican culture. For his countrymen in Morelos, Zapata was literally sanctified, and Villa too became the focus of religious cults. Even conservative governments could call upon the memories of the revolutionaries as proof of their own rectitude. Villa and Zapata became ideological symbols of the nation that everyone could appropriate. In 1931 Emiliano Zapata was declared a national hero, and his name was added to the list of illustrious Mexicans inscribed on the walls of the Chamber of Deputies in Mexico City. Pancho Villa's official recognition came later: in 1966 his name joined Zapata's, and a decade later his remains were transferred to the Monument to the revolution in Mexico City.

chapter 7

Killing the President: *John F. Kennedy*

Attention all squads. At Elm and Houston reported to be an unknown white male, approximately thirty, slender build, height five feet ten inches, 165 pounds – reported to be armed with what is believed to be a 30-calibre rifle … no further description or information at this time.[1]

Just after noon on 22 November 1963, construction worker Howard Brennan had found a space on a four-foot high wall on the corner of Houston and Elm streets in downtown Dallas from which to watch the motorcade of President John F. Kennedy as it made its way through Dealey Plaza. He checked his watch: 12.18 p.m. A few minutes later he glanced up at the building across the street, the Texas School Book Depository. In a sixth-floor window, in the south-east corner of the building, he noticed a man: 'He didn't seem to feel one bit of excitement … He seemed preoccupied,' Brennan would later recall.[2]

On the opposite side of Elm Street, about a hundred feet away from Brennan, Abraham Zapruder stood with his 8 mm cine camera. He had been thrilled to hear that the president and first lady were going to be passing his place of work as part of a two-day goodwill tour of Texas. Although the weather was now sunny and clear, it had started out cloudy, and Zapruder had initially left his camera at home. His secretary had convinced him that it was worth going back to retrieve it, and he was eagerly awaiting the arrival of the motorcade as it passed on its way to the Dallas Trade Mart, where Kennedy was due to give a speech.

John F. Kennedy and the first lady, Jacqueline – eye-catching in a vivid pink suit and matching pillbox hat – had received an enthusiastic welcome when they arrived in style at Dallas Love Field airport. Now, for travelling through the city, the president and his aides had insisted on an open-top Cadillac. He and Jackie sat on a bench seat in the back, with the governor of Texas, John Connally, and his wife, Nellie, sitting in jump seats just in front. Two Secret Service agents occupied the driver's and front passenger's seat, and four police motorcycles followed at a short distance. Behind them came more vehicles carrying Secret Service men, then a car with Vice President Lyndon B. Johnson and his wife, followed by local dignitaries and the press. The cheering crowds

President John F. Kennedy and First Lady Jackie Kennedy arrive at Dallas Love Field airport, 22 November 1963.

*The presidential motorcade passes
through downtown Dallas.*

lining the pavements had thinned out by the time the motorcade turned into Dealey Plaza, but there were still sufficient numbers to surge forward as the vehicles made their way down Houston Street, past the Old Courthouse and County Criminal Courts, before turning left into Elm Street, heading for the freeway that would take them to the trade centre. Nellie Connally turned to Kennedy to say: 'Mr President, you can't say that Dallas doesn't love you.'

At 12.30 p.m., when the president's car was about halfway down Elm Street, spectators heard what they later described as fireworks going off, or a car backfiring. Abraham Zapruder, seeing the president grab his chest, initially thought that he was playing up to the crowd,[3] but Kennedy had been shot in the back and throat, and Governor Connally had also been wounded. In the confusion the limousine slowed almost to a standstill, and Kennedy received a third shot, which destroyed the back of his head. A traumatized Jackie Kennedy, crawling onto the rear of the car, was pushed back into her seat by a Secret Service agent as the car accelerated through the underpass and sped to Parkland Memorial

Seconds after the president is struck, his traumatized wife climbs out of her seat.

Hospital. Local doctors could do nothing to save the president, who was declared dead at 1 p.m. As news of the assassination was broadcast around the world, Lyndon B. Johnson was sworn in as president on board Air Force One, shortly before it returned to Washington with Kennedy's body.

In the meantime, witnesses had led police to search the Book Depository, finding a cheap mail-order Mannlicher-Carcano rifle, three spent cartridges and one missing employee. By 1.50 p.m. a man had been arrested at a local movie theatre in connection with the murder of a police officer: this was 23-year-old Lee Harvey Oswald, who worked as a shipping clerk on the sixth floor of the Texas School Book Depository.

Newspaper headlines on a London newsstand the day after the assassination.

By the time he reached the local police station he was a prime suspect in the assassination of the president, and he was charged the following day. Oswald denied both killings, claiming that he was a 'patsy'. The next day, a police tip-off guaranteed a media frenzy as Oswald was transferred from the city to the county jail. All television cameras were focused on a faintly smirking Oswald as he was hustled through the crowd. In the crush, local nightclub owner Jack Ruby stepped forward and shot Oswald in the stomach, who died shortly after in Parkland Memorial Hospital. Ruby was arrested, later claiming that he had killed Oswald to protect Jackie from having to return to Dallas to sit through Oswald's trial.[4]

The American people were in shock. In less than twenty-four hours their president had been assassinated and his alleged murderer shot live on television. Kennedy's funeral took place on 25 November, three days after his death; the image of his veiled, grieving widow on the steps of St Matthew's Cathedral in Washington, D.C., her children by her side, was broadcast to the world. Lady Bird Johnson, who had accompanied the family from the White House, described 'a sea of faces stretching away on every side – silent, watching faces … The feeling

As Lee Harvey Oswald is transferred to the county jail, local nightclub owner Jack Ruby steps from the crowd and shoots him. The moment is broadcast live on television.

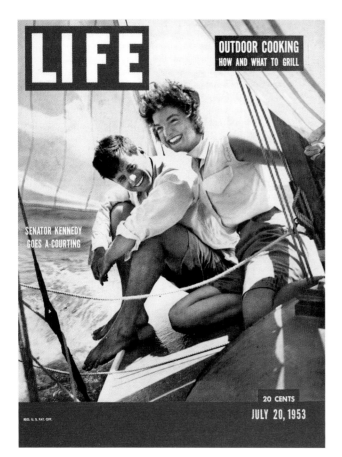

SENATOR KENNEDY
GOES A-COURTING

OUTDOOR COOKING
HOW AND WHAT TO GRILL

20 CENTS
JULY 20, 1953

The young Senator John F. Kennedy and his fiancée, Jacqueline Bouvier, sailing off the coast of Cape Cod a decade before the future president's death: the cover of LIFE magazine, 20 July 1953.

persisted that I was moving step by step through a Greek tragedy.'[5]

Almost immediately, this terrible drama entered the realms of myth. Such was the glamour and charisma of the First Family that the president was mourned by many ordinary Americans both privately, at a personal level, and on a grand scale. His death was perceived as a specifically American tragedy – one that had implications for both the country's past and its present. In America's short history, Kennedy's was the eleventh presidential assassination attempt, and the fourth to be successful. He had been shot in Dallas, a city with more murders per year than the whole of Europe combined. After the assassination it became known as the 'City of Hate', its right-wing leaders, and by extension its population, implicated in the event.

Jackie Kennedy's refusal to change out of her bloodstained suit at the swearing-in ceremony – 'Let them see what they have done,' she insisted – seemed a confirmation of the public's collective guilt. It was as though this insignificant nobody, this drop-out Oswald, could not possibly have carried the weight of responsibility alone. The gulf between this loser and the paragon that was Kennedy appeared so vast that, from the outset, it influenced – and continues to influence – all attempts to make sense of the assassination.

Kennedy's assassination was the first in the United States to be played out in the public arena, under the gaze of the modern media. It was spectacle, in a way that was unprecedented in history. The speed with which events unfolded and the violence of the imagery seemed to belong to the world of cinema or pulp fiction. Discrepancies in the initial reporting led many to believe that the truth was being withheld and that the official government version was simply an elaborate cover-up. Rather than attributing these inconsistencies to human error in a very stressful situation, many believed (then as now) that they were proof of more sinister forces at work. The initial autopsy report contained inaccuracies that were immediately seen as suspicious rather than the result of overworked doctors under pressure of time to deliver a result. The dramatic arrival of Jack Ruby in the final reel, drawing a gun with all the efficiency of a professional hitman, seemed to confirm the unreality of the event and contributed to a belief that the assassination had somehow been staged. Soon the media reporting itself became part of the unfolding drama. As newsmen gave accounts of their own experiences, they, too, became protagonists in the story. If one man's eyewitness testimony differed from those of his colleagues and rivals, it only contributed to the idea of a cover-up.

It was to counter this rising tide of conjecture that Lyndon B. Johnson commissioned an official investigation. Two days after the assassination, an internal Whitehouse memo from the deputy attorney general explicitly stated that these rumours needed to be put to rest: 'It is important that all the facts surrounding President Kennedy's Assassination be made public in a way which will satisfy people in the United States and abroad that all the facts have been told and that a statement to this effect be made now.'[6] Chaired by the chief justice of the United States, Earl Warren, the new commission held its first meeting ten days after the assassination with the brief that it should analyse all the FBI reports and interview witnesses. The outcome of this investigation was the document popularly known as the Warren Commission Report – a behemoth totalling 888 pages, with 26 accompanying volumes of evidence and testimony. Its exhaustive coverage and detailed catalogue of statements led commission member and future president Gerald Ford to describe it as 'a monumental record … a Gibraltar of factual literature'.[7] Lyndon B. Johnson was less eloquent when he was officially presented with a copy of the report on 24 September 1964: 'It's pretty heavy,' he said. It was also expensive, costing $1.2 million to produce. Initially, the commission had intended to produce a review of the FBI's criminal investigation, but contradictory evidence had led it to pursue its own enquiry. The result is based on 25,000 FBI interviews, 1,550 Secret Service interviews and 552 other interviews undertaken by the commission. The conclusion of this intensive, often repetitive and sometimes contradictory report is that Oswald, a social misfit and political malcontent, had acted alone.

Despite the commission's somewhat unsophisticated attempts at psychoanalysing Oswald (citing stereotypical explanations for his pathological behaviour, such as supposed latent homosexuality and a mother fixation), its findings fleshed out the portrait of the president's assassin as an isolated loner, one of life's losers. Born in New Orleans, Lee Harvey Oswald had

The Warren Report, submitted to President Johnson on 24 September 1964. On receiving the 888-page document, the president commented, 'It's pretty heavy.'

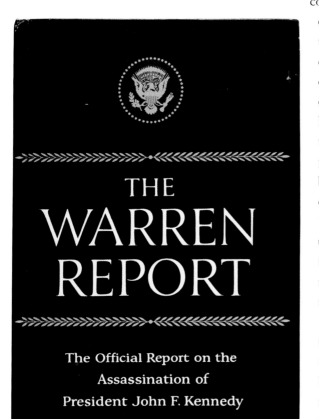

THE WARREN REPORT

The Official Report on the Assassination of President John F. Kennedy

Lee Harvey Oswald holding the rifle he used to shoot the president and a copy of the Communist Manifesto: a photograph released by the Dallas police days after the assassination. It appeared on the cover of LIFE *magazine in February 1964 and has since become known as the 'backyard photo'. Seeing discrepancies between the original and the published versions, conspiracy theorists have alleged that the photo was faked.*

had a rootless, peripatetic upbringing, raised by his mother at a series of addresses in the southern United States and in the Bronx in New York. By the time he was sixteen, truancy and petty crime had already led to a stay in a youth correctional facility in the Bronx. Disenfranchized and disaffected, he was attracted to the radicalism of the American left, and many character studies of Oswald place him in the tradition of the isolated political extremist exemplified by the self-described anarchist Leon Czolgosz, who shot President McKinley in 1901. There is another side to Oswald that does not fit this profile, however: a year after he left high school, in 1956, he joined the US Marine Corps, where he underwent standard training with a rifle. Oswald's marksmanship has been the subject of intense debate, unsurprisingly, and evidence has been offered supporting a range of abilities, from complete ineptitude to the level of a professional sniper. It can be assumed that he showed a level of competence acceptable for a US marine. During this time, Oswald learnt Russian and continued to express his communist sympathies – unusual enough for an American at the height of the cold war, and extraordinary for a marine. By October 1959 he had left the Marines and defected to Russia, planning, with a deluded sense of the value of his information, to pass on military intelligence he had acquired during his training. He ended up far from the hub of political activity, in Minsk, where he worked in an electronics factory and eventually married a Russian woman. After three years of life in the Soviet Union he became disillusioned and made arrangements to return to the United States with his wife, securing visas in 1962.

What happened in the eighteenth months between Oswald's arrival back in the United States and the death of the president? On his return, Oswald renewed his involvement with left-wing American organizations, including communist and pro-Cuban groups. The Warren Commission would paint a picture of Oswald as a political radical, using as evidence letters from Oswald to his wife concerning an assassination attempt on Major General Edwin Walker, a vehement supporter of racial segregation and leader of the far-right John Bircher Society; doubts have since been cast over the extent of Oswald's involvement both in the assassination attempt and in far-left politics. In the immediate aftermath of Kennedy's assassination, many believed that the president had been the target of far-right extremists. That hypothesis was abandoned when Oswald's dealings with the Soviet Union became known, only for it to be picked up once again by later conspiracy theorists, who believed that Oswald actively took part in far-right meetings several months after Walker's attempted shooting.

Both official and unofficial research into the assassination has been united by the need to construct a mythology around Lee Harvey Oswald. This is because if Oswald's life had no meaning, there would be no meaning in Kennedy's death. Conspiracy theorists construct such meaning by viewing Oswald as part of a much wider web of intrigue – an insignificant foot soldier, perhaps, but one who represents an amazingly sophisticated network, the tip of a vast iceberg of conspiracy. On the other hand, official accounts that have concluded Oswald acted alone, such as the Warren Commission, seem compelled to find proof of Oswald's uniqueness in order to explain how he was capable of such an act. For the United States government, the reasons for emphasizing his singularity were twofold: first, it avoided the need to ask uncomfortable questions about what kind of country creates citizens capable of murdering its heads of state. If Oswald was a one-off, a lone madman with peculiar pathologies, he was not a product of American society in general, nor could he be seen to represent a particular kind of American behaviour. Second, and most importantly, to have felled the most powerful man in

the world, Oswald himself must have possessed some preternatural qualities. For if Oswald's act were nothing more than the fury of an aggrieved individual, it would diminish Kennedy's death, and indeed his life. Jackie Kennedy herself gave voice to this theory, reflecting on how Oswald's very inconsequentiality seemed to rob the president's death of any meaning. 'He didn't even have the satisfaction of being killed for civil rights ... it had to be some silly little Communist,' she said.[8]

A widespread refusal to believe in the influence of 'some silly little Communist', combined with a distrust of authority in general – one that took root with the assassination and has flourished ever since – has led to a hydra-like body of conspiracy theories that has taken on a life of its own, seeming to grow only more vigorous and complex the further the event recedes into the past. At the time of the assassination, only 29 per cent of Americans believed that Oswald had acted alone; the rest blamed a range of other suspects, including the Mafia, Fidel Castro, the Soviet Union, the far right in the United States, and African-Americans. High-profile figures such as Malcolm X fuelled the flames when he described the assassination as 'chickens coming home to roost', claiming that Kennedy had been assassinated because of US foreign policy (a controversial sentiment that resurfaced after the 9/11 attacks on the World Trade Center). Even before the Warren Commission had published its official findings, the public became aware of inconsistencies in the various accounts of the assassination, leading to doubts that have never been dispersed. The initial autopsy report, which was prepared under extremely difficult circumstances, described the wound to Kennedy's throat as compatible with an entry wound, contributing to a belief that Kennedy was shot from the front as well as from behind. Questions arose concerning the number of shots that had been fired; three spent cartridges were found in the Depository, yet investigators believed that they had found evidence of four bullets. This story was backed up by witnesses who claimed to have heard more than three gunshots, although it appeared that Dealey Plaza was as an 'echo chamber' that would have distorted the sound of gunfire. Chaotic press conferences seemed to contradict information provided only days earlier. Once the Warren Report had been published and backed by the mainstream press, however, faith in the official 'lone gunman' theory was restored, albeit briefly, with 87 per cent of the population accepting the government's version of events. However, just a few years later, after the Watergate scandal and with trust in the authorities at an all-time low, conspiracy theories once more gained ground. Later they became further entrenched in the public's consciousness with the release of Oliver

Jackie Kennedy flanked by her two children at John F. Kennedy's state funeral. The moving image of 3-year-old John Kennedy, Jr., saluting his father's coffin as it proceeded down Pennsylvania Avenue was published around the world. Over 300,000 mourners lined the route.

Stone's film *JFK* in 1991, a conspiracist retelling of the assassination that mixes fact with fiction to a confusing degree and that has undoubtedly influenced the way we approach and understand the event today – thus providing ample demonstration of the power of popular media to rewrite history. Today, a belief in some element of conspiracy far outweighs any trust in the official version of events: it is reported that between three-quarters and four-fifths of Americans are suspicious of the government report. Even President Johnson, who at the time publicly backed the findings of the commission and praised the exhaustive work that had gone into it, privately believed that Kennedy's death was connected to a secret CIA project to assassinate foreign leaders, of which he had been unaware until becoming president himself.

Central to all conspiracy theories is the film shot by Abraham Zapruder: described as the 'Rosetta Stone' for all who see an underlying plot,[9] it is adduced as counter-evidence to the findings of the Warren Commission. This brief footage is, for those who doubt the official version of events, as packed with evidence as the almost pathologically detailed Warren Report. Purely by chance, Abraham Zapruder had been almost directly opposite Kennedy's car when the shots were fired. He had been filming the motorcade as it came down Elm Street but stopped when he realized that the approaching cars were only preliminary vehicles, resuming again with the arrival of the president. The resulting 26.6 seconds of colour film capture the moment of impact and provide the clearest visual record of the assassination, presenting an almost unimpeded view (there is a brief moment when the car is blocked by a freeway sign). Immediately following the shooting, a horrified Zapruder hurried back to his office, evidently in shock: 'They killed him! They killed him!', he repeated to the arriving crowds who were unaware of what had just happened. Within an hour, word of his film had reached the local Secret Service, who arrived at his office along with several journalists. The film was developed, and the Secret Service took two copies as evidence; the images were subsequently reproduced as stills and included in the Warren Commission Report. By the following day, the major news agencies had descended on Zapruder, each bidding for the rights to reproduce the film.

Zapruder's footage is so well known today that many believe it was televised at the time of the assassination; in fact, it was not broadcast in its entirety until 1975. Its release contributed to a reopening of the assassination inquiry by Congress that same year. In the immediate aftermath of Kennedy's death the film was felt to be too disturbing for public consumption, and Abraham Zapruder, respectful of the material's sensitive nature, immediately voiced concerns that without tight controls bootleg copies could end up at 'sleazy Time Square movie houses'.[10] In the event, an exclusive deal was negotiated with *LIFE* magazine, a leading illustrated weekly, which reproduced 31 of the 486 frames in black and white as part of a special issue devoted to the assassination. This series was carefully selected to convey the moments of tragedy without including the most explicit frames. It was not until the publication of the Warren Commission Report that the entire sequence was made available to the public.

Analysis of the footage has itself filled many volumes. The original film – grainy, flickering and silent – has undergone painstaking scientific examination; each frame has been obsessively scrutinized and enlarged to the point of abstraction, rendering any indistinct shape or shadowy form in the background both unreadable and infinitely permeable. 'Depending on your point of view, it proves almost anything you want it to prove,' commented the editor of *LIFE* magazine, Richard Stolley, and indeed it has been used by both conspiracy theorists and those who back the official report to prove their respective cases.

Conspiracy theorists made much of the sharp backward movement of the president's head as he received the first shot, citing it as proof that a bullet must have come from the front. Whatever else the film may prove or disprove, it illustrates the potency of visual evidence; it confirms what we believe to be true (wouldn't something need to be struck from the front to make it move backwards?) rather than what we know to be true (how many of us have actually seen someone shot in the head?), and appears to provide an irrefutable record of reality. In truth, the tiny size of the original image makes it very difficult to establish what is happening with any certainty; and at the crucial firing of the first shot the car is concealed behind a freeway sign. The first time the footage was shown on television in the United States, an accompanying commentary told the viewers what they were seeing. Without such an explanation it is difficult to make sense of what is happening, yet the commentary leads the viewer into seeing what is being described, and prevents any alternative understanding or interpretation of what is being played out.

On the official side, recent three-dimensional computer-generated imagery based on the film footage has provided compelling evidence supporting the 'lone gunman' theory.[11] The Warren Commission's findings point to a single bullet hitting both the president and the governor, which conspiracy theorists dismiss as a 'magic bullet', whose trajectory would have had to defy time and gravity to hit two men. The computer reconstruction, however, provides evidence to support the

overleaf A still from the Zapruder film, showing Jackie Kennedy attempting to support the president as the second bullet strikes. Abraham Zapruder, who captured the moment of the assassination entirely by accident on a home movie camera, was concerned from the outset that if the material were made public it might become a target for sensationalist voyeurism.

Warren Report: the governor is sitting on a jump seat, lower than the president – not at the same height, as the Zapruder footage would seem to suggest. It is thus entirely feasible for a single bullet to have hit both men. However, in an endless round of argument and counter-argument, some conspiracy theorists now assert that the Zapruder footage is itself an elaborate forgery, citing, in an example of looking-glass logic, the very fact that it upholds the government's official version as proof of its falsity – just one more example of the tortuous lengths the government was prepared to go to hide 'the truth' about the assassination.

Conspiracy beliefs about the Kennedy assassination in this way both reflect and feed into the growth of conspiracy theories in general in the United States. Since the 1960s they have gradually merged together, creating a vast umbrella of imagined plots that all reflect a distrust of authority in general. From this standpoint, Kennedy's presidency is seen to symbolize a distant, golden age in which the people trusted their head of state. His death, long regarded as the moment when America 'lost its innocence', thus imbues Kennedy's life with a sense of integrity, of purity almost, that his successors could not attain; indeed, many came to represent the very authorities that destroyed him.

The United States was to receive two further blows with the assassinations of Martin Luther King, Jr., and Robert F. Kennedy in 1968.

The scene on a Memphis motel balcony moments after the assassination of Martin Luther King, Jr., on 4 April 1968. King's death, and that of Senator Robert F. Kennedy that same year, prompted President Lyndon B. Johnson to convene the National Committee on the Causes and Prevention of Violence (NCCPV) to study aspects of violence in America.

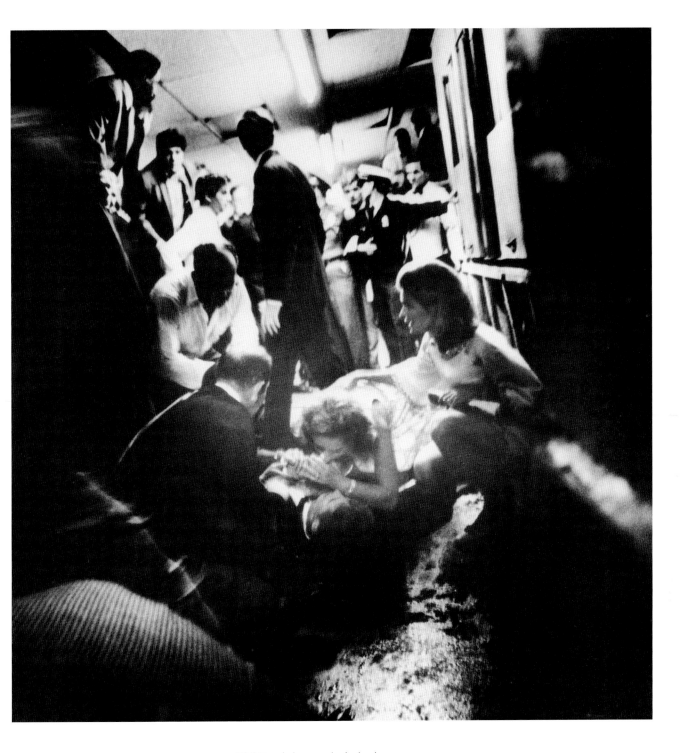

Ethel Kennedy leans over her husband,
Robert F. Kennedy, after his shooting in the
Ambassador Hotel, Los Angeles, 5 June
1968. Sirhan Sirhan, a 24-year-old
Palestinian immigrant, had felt betrayed
by Kennedy's support of Israel during the
Six-Day War. He had written in his diary:
'My determination to eliminate RFK is
becoming more and more of an unshakable
obsession. RFK must die.'

Less than a week after the murder of Robert F. Kennedy on 5 June, President Johnson convened the National Committee on the Causes and Prevention of Violence (NCCPV), comprising a group of young lawyers organized into separate 'task forces' each focusing on different aspects of violence in America. The resulting report has been described as a 'science of assassinology'. Much broader in scope than the detail-obsessed Warren Report, the document looked at the social, political and historical conditions that led to assassinations. It concluded that, shocking as Kennedy's assassination was, it was far from unprecedented in the country's history: the United States has witnessed attacks against its presidents since the early 19th century, particularly (and, in retrospect, not surprisingly) during times of political and social turmoil. To date there have been sixteen assassination attempts, of which four have been successful; and since Kennedy's death every president except Johnson has had at least one attempt made on his life. The NCCPV report concluded that the 'lone gunman', too, had a historical precedent, both in the form of individuals such as Leon Czolgosz, President McKinley's assassin, and as an archetype. The ideals of individualism, frontier justice and the right to bear arms are deeply embedded within the mythology of America's founding, and all seem to converge in the figure of the vigilante, who metes out his own justice. Writ large, this means that the aggrieved individual takes his complaint to the very top, to the head of state.

The NCCPV also found that, of the assassinations that had taken place that decade, the public had been most deeply affected by 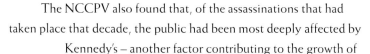 Kennedy's – another factor contributing to the growth of conspiracy theories. Bereavement is often accompanied by a sense of disbelief, and these theories are in many ways a distortion of our natural need to make sense of the incomprehensible. Although Kennedy's assassination is a landmark in the growth of conspiracy theories, the public's reaction to his death is not unprecedented: when Abraham Lincoln was shot by John Wilkes Booth on Good Friday 1865 while attending a theatre performance, immediate parallels were drawn with Christ's martyrdom. The more saintly Lincoln became in retrospect, the larger the plot required to cut down such a paragon. It comes as no surprise that this first presidential assassination in America's history also spawned the first – and now the longest-running – presidential assassination conspiracy theories: among other

John Wilkes Booth leaps onto the stage of Ford's Theatre, Washington, D.C., after shooting President Abraham Lincoln, 14 April 1865. Lincoln was the first American president to be assassinated.

alleged perpetrators, it points to leaders of the Confederate South, Lincoln's successor, Andrew Johnson, and even the papacy. Lincoln's assassin, however, clearly saw himself as continuing a legacy of heroic endeavour that stretched back to antiquity. Booth held Lincoln responsible for the Civil War ('Our country owed all her troubles to him'), and his last diary entry refers to his individual bravery and self-sacrifice for the greater good of the country ('God simply made me the instrument of [Lincoln's] punishment'). Following his attack on the president, Booth leapt on the theatre's stage crying 'Sic semper tyrannis!' ('Thus always to tyrants!') before making his escape. He seemed genuinely surprised when his actions were not met with national rejoicing, writing of being 'hunted like a dog ... for doing what Brutus was honored for'. Booth was pursued by regimental soldiers to a farm in

Virginia, where he was shot and subsequently died from his wounds. A series of popular legends claiming that he had evaded capture – some circulating before he had even been shot – and alleged sightings of the wanted man in various cities for decades to follow attest to the powerful myths that develop around the figure of the assassin. Booth may have seen himself as a righteous avenger; his horrified countrymen, however, saw him as a bogeyman with almost supernatural abilities to defy capture. As a bizarre coda to the story, what was purported to be his mummified corpse was an enduring attraction in carnival sideshows during the Depression era.

Booth's political motives may have been overlooked, but the assassin of President McKinley in 1901 – Leon Czolgosz, a factory worker of Polish descent from Detroit – explained his intentions very clearly, admitting that the reasons for the killing were entirely political. (He made a dramatic eleventh-hour statement as he was being strapped into the electric chair, crying out: 'I killed the President because he was the enemy of the good people! I did it for the help of the good people, the working men of all countries!') Nonetheless, at his trial the defence made a plea of insanity, which brought to public attention the plight of immigrants, the dangers of capitalism and the shadowy threat of international anarchism. Czolgosz's working-class, immigrant status made him acutely aware of the dark side of the American capitalist dream embodied by President McKinley's administration. Inspired by the speeches of the anarchist Emma Goldman, he had become involved in local anarchist groups, but his social awkwardness and his belief in government conspiracies led to his increasing isolation. Nonetheless, his desire to improve the conditions

below *President William McKinley arrives at the Pan-American Exposition of 1901 in Buffalo, New York. Following the shooting, doctors were initially confident of the president's recovery, but he died eight days later of complications from the bullet still lodged in his body. The X-ray machine, exhibited at the Exposition for the first time, might have saved his life, but doctors were afraid to risk using it.*

below right *Crowds await President McKinley's funeral procession in the rain, Washington, D.C.*

LESLIE'S WEEKLY

McKINLEY EXTRA

Vol. XCIII.—EXTRA NUMBER.
Copyright, 1901, by Judge Company, No. 110 Fifth Avenue

New York, September 9, 1901

PRICE 10 CENTS
Entered as second-class matter at the New York Post-Office

LEON F. CZOLGOSZ, THE ASSASSIN.

FIRST PHOTOGRAPH OF THE WRETCHED ANARCHIST WHO SHOT THE PRESIDENT AT FOUR P. M., SEPTEMBER 6TH, 1901, AT THE PAN-AMERICAN
EXPOSITION.—COPYRIGHTED BY JUDGE COMPANY, 1901.

of the working man continued to grow and eventually led him to Buffalo, New York, at the time that McKinley was visiting the Pan-American Exposition. On 6 September Czolgosz joined a crowd on the steps of Buffalo's Temple of Music as the president greeted well-wishers. Holding a pistol concealed in a white handkerchief, Czolgosz approached the president as if to shake his hand, and shot him twice. McKinley died of his wounds eight days later, a bullet still lodged in his body. Czolgosz, badly beaten by the president's security guards, narrowly missed a lynching by the crowd. He spoke little at his trial, seemingly unable to understand some of the questions put to him, but stated briefly: 'There was no one else but me. No one else told me to do it, and no one paid me to do it.' The plea of insanity entered on his behalf cited a mental breakdown in 1898, brought about by extreme social deprivation. Czolgosz was found guilty and sentenced to death by electrocution.

If any assassination can be said to have changed history, McKinley's at least brought to public attention the social conditions of America's immigrant poor and paved the way for the policies of his successor, Theodore Roosevelt, and the Progressive Era. Whether Czolgosz was a rational anarchist, threatening to undermine American freedoms, or a victim of those same freedoms, his case raised questions about individual versus state responsibility.

Kennedy's assassination offers no such retrospective salve. Without the assassin's testimony there can be no debate based on motive, and no collective examination of societal or political responsibility. Instead, the Kennedy assassination now stands as the point at which the United States government lost the trust of its public, a situation that continued for decades. This attitude is visible in a widespread refusal to wholly accept the official government line on just about anything, and is amply demonstrated by public's reaction to the attacks on the World Trade Center.

And yet belief in conspiracies is also perversely comforting. It allows us to attempt to piece together and make sense of the otherwise unfathomable. William Manchester, the author of one of the first books about the Kennedy assassination, described this need: 'If you put the murdered President of the United States on one side of a scale and that wretched waif Oswald on the other side, it doesn't balance. You want to add something weightier to Oswald. It would invest the President's death with meaning, endowing him with martyrdom. He would have died for *something*. A conspiracy, would, of course, do the job nicely.'

Conspiracy theories and beliefs in official cover-ups have become so enmeshed in the story of Kennedy's death that no commentary about

the event can ever be entirely free of them. To date, over one thousand books have been written on the subject, many based on amateur investigations. There is a thriving conference and seminar circuit based on such 'grassroots' scholarship, in which new and old theories are presented, argued, disproven and reconfirmed in a seemingly endless cycle. These findings have become part of popular consciousness in the United States, so that today over three-quarters of Americans believe that the authorities were involved in some kind of cover-up. As the incident becomes more distant, so does the likelihood of finding a definitive answer.

The effects of the assassination still influence American culture. Initially, the events of 22 November 1963 added impetus to the CIA's anti-Castro campaign, which attempted to follow the fraying thread of Lee Harvey Oswald's communist sympathies all the way to the Cuban premier, resulting in the often laughable cloak-and-dagger antics of Operation Mongoose. In the longer term, they introduced the idea that the government was not to be trusted. The mass of evidence unearthed by the Warren Commission inadvertently revealed a sinister side to the US military—industrial complex that the public had previously been unaware of. The faith that the American public had in the motives of its government before Kennedy's assassination was now irrevocably lost.

chapter 8

State-Sanctioned Plots: *Assassination as Foreign Policy*

The assassinations discussed up to this point have for the most part been the work of lone individuals or small groups on the margins of power. Their aims have been to disrupt the status quo, to right perceived wrongs, to overthrow a tyrant, or to draw attention to specific grievances, real or imagined. What they all assumed is that their actions would in some way bring about their desired aims: a just and lawful government; public attention for their plight or cause; or, in the case of the anarchists, a destruction of the status quo. The validity of this assumption has been constantly questioned: 'The tyranny survives though the tyrant is dead,' wrote Cicero; 'Assassination has never changed the history of the world,' Benjamin Disraeli agreed nearly two millennia later. Most often, assassination appears to be the last act of a desperate individual than a coherent political strategy. But what if a government employs assassination as an active part of its foreign policy? The adoption of such tactics sends a clear signal not only that assassination can be justified, but also that it works; that by removing one key figure the whole edifice of the state will come crashing down. Nowhere is the belief in assassination's efficacy more evident than in the activities of the US Central Intelligence Agency during the cold war.

The CIA was established under the administration of President Truman in 1947, in the cold war's early days. Its remit was to gather, analyse and disseminate foreign intelligence that might affect national security. Under the provision of the National Security Act of 1947, the CIA was subject to control by the US president and the National Security Council, and it was prohibited from carrying out law enforcement activities. Yet as the cold war progressed, the Agency's policies became increasingly interventionist, and the organization itself acted more and more as an autonomous unit, seemingly answerable to no one. Its more heavy-handed tactics drew comparison with those of its Soviet counterpart, the KGB, which had originally been founded to concentrate on domestic affairs but by the late 1950s was, like the CIA, increasingly active in foreign affairs. The KGB's predecessor, the NKVD, had been behind the assassination of the exiled Leon Trotsky in Mexico in 1940. During the cold war, the KGB carried out assassinations abroad,

Fidel Castro seems amused at newspaper revelations of an assassination plot against him, April 1959.

Leon and Natalia Trotsky arriving at Tampico, Mexico, in January 1937. Trotsky lived in exile in Mexico until he was assassinated on 20 August 1940 by Ramon Mercador, an agent sent by the Soviets.

but they targeted Soviet defectors. Despite conspiracy theories that linked Lee Harvey Oswald to the KGB, or rumours of a Soviet plot to assassinate Pope John Paul II in 1981, no evidence has been found. During this period, however, the CIA is known to have plotted the assassination of several foreign leaders and, even if it was not directly responsible for pulling the proverbial trigger, to have aided political coups that were certain to end in death for the toppled heads of state. In the 1960s and early 1970s, during the administrations of presidents Kennedy, Johnson and Nixon, the chain of command became ever more convoluted – which in itself became part of Agency policy and which would raise questions about the extent of the president's knowledge in Agency affairs. The CIA maintained a policy of 'plausible deniability', in which obfuscation, euphemism, innuendo and doublespeak were employed as tactics in its covert operations against foreign leaders believed to be inimical to US interests. This approach allowed more than enough room in which to manoeuvre should it become necessary to deny

The emblem of the CIA.

Richard Nixon congratulates the newly sworn-in President John F. Kennedy, with Vice President Lyndon B. Johnson looking on. The activities of the CIA under the Kennedy and, later, the Johnson administrations came under the scrutiny of the Church Committee.

the involvement, or indeed the prior knowledge, of the president. As a Senate investigation into the alleged assassination plots of the period concluded in 1975,[1] whether the order for assassinations came directly from the president, whether he had no knowledge of them at all, or whether the truth lay somewhere in between, the use of assassination as a tool of foreign policy would do untold damage to America's reputation in the rest of the world. As one commentator noted, the Agency's biggest mistake was to move from intelligence to intervention – as was demonstrated by its campaign against Fidel Castro during the 1960s.

The arrival of Fidel Castro and his army in Havana on 1 January 1959 had ended the right-wing dictatorship of Fulgencio Batista. By mid-February Castro was sworn in as Cuba's new prime minister, attracting the intense scrutiny of the CIA. Alarmed both by the possibility that Castro's socialism would spread to the rest of Latin America, and by the fact that Cuba itself would become a satellite of the Soviet Union only 90 miles from America's shores, the CIA initiated an official programme against the Cuban premier. Its tactics

ranged from undermining his credibility among his supporters, to his recommended 'elimination',[2] to everything in between. As an illustration of the often absurd and surreal lengths the CIA was prepared to go to achieve its aims, the crusade against Castro is a perfect case study. It also highlighted just how murky the lines of communication were between the Agency and the United States president.

Between 1960 and 1965 the CIA worked overtime in devising plots to topple Castro. Following the failed Bay of Pigs invasion in April 1961 by Cuban exiles aiming to overthrow Castro, President John F. Kennedy authorized an aggressive CIA campaign against him codenamed Operation Mongoose. The removal of Castro became, as several commentators have noted, almost an obsession with the president and his brother, Senator Robert F. Kennedy. If this is the case, it certainly goes some way to explain the fantastical – and also the highly personal – nature of some of the plots against the Cuban premier. An independent US report into the CIA's activities admits to at least eight plots to assassinate Castro, although his supporters claim that there

Fidel Castro enters Havana after the toppling of the Batista government on 1 January 1959. When Castro declared himself to be a Marxist-Leninist one year later, relations with the US became increasingly tense.

Fidel Castro jumps from a tank at Girón, near the Bay of Pigs, in April 1961. The US attempt to invade Cuba and overthrow the Communist regime using CIA-trained Cuban exiles was a failure.

were over six hundred, either by the CIA or by Cuban exiles in the United States.[3] Whether the principal aim was to discredit Castro or to kill him, some of the plots were positively bizarre in their details. One of the main strategies was to attack Castro the symbol rather than Castro the man. In an approach that has been described as peculiarly American for its focus on surface image, the CIA planned to undermine Castro as if credible leadership were simply a question of appearance. Proposed methods included sprinkling his shoes with a powerful depilatory in the hope of destroying his famous beard and, along with it, his Latin machismo. Another idea was to lace his cigars with LSD just before a public appearance, so that the premier's clearly disoriented performance would destroy the nation's confidence in his abilities. (The use of cigars resurfaced in one of the assassination plots, in which it was suggested that a box of cigars filled with explosives should be left near Castro at a state function. Quite apart from the cartoonish aspect of exploding cigars, the idea was dropped over concerns that someone other than Castro might smoke them.) A more oblique attack on the Cuban leader was put forward in a plot involving speedboats off the coast of Havana, from which fireworks would rain down pamphlets heralding the Second Coming and bearing a message from the new messiah to beware of bearded men. Such ludicrous schemes clearly did nothing but discredit the CIA at home, and by extension the United States abroad, when they were made public in the mid-1970s.

More serious in intent, although hardly in method, were the plots to kill Castro. The CIA seemed to waver between elaborately concocted scenarios straight out of a boy's adventure story and the crudeness of hiring mafia hitmen to attack the leader in a blaze of gunfire. (These hired assassins, allegedly, were disappointed not to be able to benefit from the high-tech methods available to the CIA.) Many of these plans did not advance beyond the walls of the testing laboratory, but they revealed a baroque imagination at work that possessed an intimate knowledge of Castro's habits. He was known to scuba dive, so one suggestion was to plant a brightly painted shell filled with explosives in his favourite diving spot, which would detonate when it was retrieved from the seabed. Another was to sprinkle the spores of a chronic skin disease into his diving suit, or to infect the breathing apparatus with the tuberculosis bacteria. Not surprisingly, given the overwhelming impression that these plots were devised by a group of overgrown boys in their secret den, they did not progress beyond the theory stage. Those that did tended to be of the old-fashioned variety, involving guns and mobsters – the proverbial dirty tricks carried out by dirty people. In the late summer of 1963, Castro announced publicly that he knew of the CIA plots against him. The last attempt on his life under the Kennedy administration was made on 22 November of that year, the day that the American president was assassinated. Oswald's links with the US Communist Party and Castro's public acknowledgment of Operation Mongoose led to President Lyndon B. Johnson establishing the House Select Committee on Assassinations to investigate Kennedy's death. Despite the exhaustive findings of the Warren Commission, and its conclusion that Lee Harvey Oswald was a lone assassin, Johnson continued to suspect that Castro had been responsible for Kennedy's murder, believing that the CIA's use of assassination against foreign leaders had prompted a revenge killing.

President Johnson's suspicions highlight one of the fundamental problems with assassination as foreign policy: the very real possibility that it might provoke a similar strike in retaliation . When the CIA's activities progressed from intelligence-gathering to intervention, the covert nature of its activities became more and more suspect, casting a shadow on the United States' worldwide reputation. But, quite apart

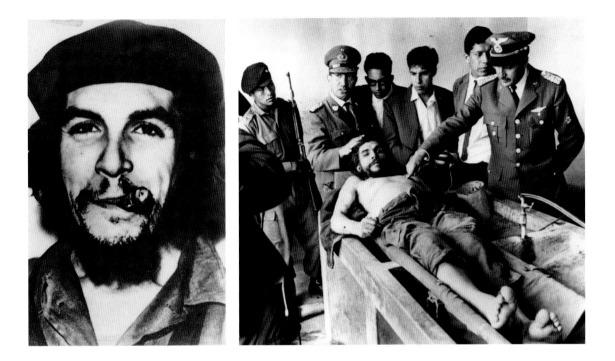

Che Guevara, icon of the left, had met Raúl and Fidel Castro in Mexico in 1955. After his killing in 1967 by Bolivian soldiers in concert with the CIA, his corpse was put on ignominious display in the laundry of Vallegrande hospital. During its investigations the Church Committee found evidence that, in the early 1960s, the CIA had used, in the committee's words, 'terminology … suggesting that the assassination of Castro, his brother Raúl, and Che Guevara was at least theoretically considered'.

from any potential fall-out for the United States should assassins be discovered, assassination as a tactic was itself flawed at the most basic level. It assumed that the head of state *was* the state. Remove Castro, the reasoning ran, and socialist Cuba would be no more. America had only to look at its own history of presidential assassinations to know that this was untrue; nonetheless, the dirty tricks campaign continued, and Castro was not the only world leader to be targeted by the CIA.

In early 1960, shortly after CIA heads had begun recommending the 'elimination' of Castro, President Eisenhower called for an extension of their remit. The deposed Batista was now in the Dominican Republic, but Eisenhower's advisors focused their attention on the country's right-wing dictator, Rafael Leónidas Trujillo. Although Trujillo was vehemently anti-Castro, his regime's appalling track record of corruption, murder and terrorism was not one the United States wished to be associated with; in this instance the 'enemy of my enemy' was clearly not a friend. 'Trujillo', an advisor on Latin American affairs told President Eisenhower at a meeting in May 1960, 'is involved in all sorts of efforts all over the hemisphere to create disorder.' A transcript of the discussion revealed that the president thought Castro, too, was a troublemaker, and that he 'would like to see them both sawed off'.[4] As the Church Committee would later reveal, the CIA's use of innuendo often left the extent of the president's knowledge of or complicity in the CIA's assassination programme open to question. In the case of Trujillo, however, there is

Vice President Richard Nixon and General Rafael Leónidas Trujillo of the Dominican Republic greet each other on Nixon's arrival in Ciudad Trujillo (Santo Domingo), 1 March 1955. The involvement of the CIA in the dictator's assassination has been suspected but remains unproven.

enough evidence to prove President Eisenhower's approval. The actual facts surrounding Trujillo's death are murky. He was killed in a hail of machine-gun fire by seven assailants – not the usual modus operandi of the Latin American tyrannicide, according to one expert.[5] The findings of the Church Committee, which examined this and other assassinations of the 1970s, were inconclusive; it decided that, although the United States had engaged in plots against Trujillo, there was not enough evidence to prove it that had connections with his killers at the time of his death. But whether or not the United States was responsible in this case, assassination was now a recognized and 'acceptable' CIA tactic.

Eisenhower's knowledge and/or sanction of the programme pursued in the Congo are more ambiguous still. In August 1960 a telegram reached Washington from the CIA chief in Leopoldville warning that the newly independent Democratic Republic of Congo was in danger of becoming 'another Cuba'.[6] In the month after it had gained independence from Belgium, on 30 June of that year, the country had seen widespread unrest. The national army, the Force Publique, had mutinied, killing its Belgian officers, and a period of complete anarchy followed, with extensive looting and escalating danger to civilians. Any Belgians still in the country soon fled, and by 14 July 1960 the UN Security Council made a decision to intervene. The United States, concerned that the Soviet Union would attempt to turn the chaos to its advantage, looked for a way to restore a semblance of order and soon found its target: the newly elected prime minister, Patrice Lumumba, whose policy of pro-African, anticolonial activism was now viewed by the West as vulnerable to Communist intervention.

Fifteen years later, the Church Committee would investigate the extent of American responsibility for Lumumba's death, but on 18 August 1960, when the US National Security Council met in Washington to discuss the deteriorating situation, the then CIA director Allen Dulles came away from the meeting concluding that he had Eisenhower's authority to assassinate the prime minister. The president had called for 'strong action' and recommended that the only course of action was to 'remove' Lumumba from the scene at the earliest possibility. Many hours and many dollars would later be spent attempting to interpret the president's words, but at the time the CIA began to put a plan into action. Shortly afterwards, the CIA chief in Leopoldville received a consignment of items from the United States, including hypodermic needles, surgical masks, rubber gloves and a deadly toxin to slip into Lumumba's food or toothpaste. As with the plots against Castro, the assassins who were hired to carry out the deed came from the criminal underworld – men whose allegiances could be bought and whose morality was reasonably elastic. The findings of the Church Committee make reference to a particular agent recommended by the CIA's Africa division because:

> He is indeed aware of the precepts of right and wrong, but if he is given an assignment which may be morally wrong in the eyes of the world, but necessary because his case officer ordered him to carry it out, then it is right, and he will dutifully undertake appropriate action for its execution without pangs of conscience. In a word, he can rationalize all actions.[7]

The report tersely concludes that 'this rationalization is not in keeping with the ideals of our nation'.[8] But, at the time, the slippery path of communication between the various departments of the White House allowed for some creative interpretations of meaning, from the highest authority down.

The 007-style poisoned toothpaste plot was never carried out because events in the Congo escalated before it could be put into place. On 17 January 1961, Lumumba was seized by soldiers and flown to the province of Katanga. The mine-rich region had recently declared its independence from the rest of the Congo, and its president, Moise Tombe, was Lumumba's sworn enemy. The prime minister's arrest was essentially a death warrant. When he and the two aides arrested with him disembarked in Katanga, they were pistol-whipped by soldiers, dragged

The deposed Patrice Lumumba, with hands tied behind his back, at Leopoldville airport under a guard of Congolese soldiers. He was murdered six weeks later.

off in an army convoy and killed some time later. Despite rumours that Lumumba had been murdered, the CIA kept their own agent in situ until they were satisfied that he was no longer required. Lumumba's death was not officially announced until February of that year.

Although no US agent had pulled a trigger or injected a toxin, America's involvement in the Congo was extremely damaging to its reputation abroad and led to a wave of anti-American feeling. Lumumba's murder was the first of a series of political assassinations in sub-Saharan Africa during the first half of the 1960s, in which many were the victims of military coups.[9] A few short years later, in 1966, Lumumba's enemies were hailing him as a martyr for African independence, the victim of colonial despotism.[10]

President Eisenhower's call for 'strong action' in the Democratic Republic of Congo was open to interpretation; equally ambiguous was John F. Kennedy's attitude to the South Vietnamese president Ngo Dinh

Diem and his brother, Ngo Dinh Nhu, the chief of the secret police. These two brothers were killed in a coup d'état three weeks before the assassination of President Kennedy, but the question of whether the United States had prior knowledge of the revolt was contentious. Certainly, news neither of the coup nor of the brothers' assassinations caused any grief in Washington, but the 1975 Church Report would investigate how far the United States could be viewed as culpable. Kennedy had categorically forbidden any American involvement, and yet a National Security advisor, McGeorge Bundy, recalled the exasperated president alluding to Henry II's 'turbulent priest' phrase before the death of Thomas Becket, with equally ambiguous meaning.[11] Kennedy's successor, Lyndon B. Johnson, was convinced that the CIA's involvement in assassination plots had led to Kennedy's death, and that his own life might be in danger for the same motive of revenge. His suspicion that Castro had been involved in his predecessor's assassination was well known, but the CIA agent and future director Richard Helms made a telling remark at the time that shed light on America's involvement in Vietnam: he quoted Johnson as saying that Kennedy had died because of his involvement in Ngo Dinh Diem's assassination.[12]

The CIA did not target only heads of state. From mid-1967, as the Vietcong's bid for South Vietnam intensified, the Agency decided to focus all US intelligence efforts on investigating the army's infrastructure.

At Washington airport, President Eisenhower chats amicably with Ngo Dinh Diem, president of South Vietnam, 8 May 1957. Six years later Diem was assassinated during a CIA-led coup d'état.

*President Charles de Gaulle greeting
crowds in Brittany, January 1969.
An estimated thirty-three attempts were
made on his life, including a plot in
which an assassin was to shake his hand
while wearing a poisoned ring.*

The result was the Saigon-based Operation Phoenix. Its aim was
to identify and, in Washington's terminology, to 'neutralize' local
Vietcong leaders. Engaging once again in verbal acrobatics, the CIA
never spelled out the precise meaning of 'neutralize', but the reality
of its policy was the capture and death of Vietcong activists, often in
a hail of bullets. It was not clear whether any other strategy had been
intended or even planned, and certainly no others were employed.
Although the killings may have been carried out by Vietnamese
personnel, American agents pulled the strings. Operation Phoenix
was a bloody, self-defeating mess, which caused the deaths of around
20,000 Vietcong leaders and sympathizers.

President Johnson may have feared reprisals for the Agency's
attacks on foreign leaders, but that did not stop the CIA pursuing similar
tactics under his own administration. In 1975 the *Chicago Tribune* reported

the CIA's links to an assassination attempt on the oft-targeted (as many as thirty times) French president Charles de Gaulle a decade earlier:

> *Congressional leaders have been told of Central Intelligence Agency involvement in a plot by French dissidents to assassinate the late French President Charles De Gaulle ... Sometime in the mid-1960s – probably in 1965 or 1966 – dissidents in the De Gaulle government are said to have made contact with the CIA to seek help in a plot to murder the French leader ... A hired assassin, armed with a poison ring, was to be slipped into a crowd of old soldiers of France, when General De Gaulle was to be the host at a reception.* [13]

De Gaulle was no favourite of the Johnson administration, and the feeling was reciprocated. His demands that the United States should withdraw its forces from the former French colony of Indochina enraged Washington, and for his part de Gaulle was convinced that the CIA had been responsible for the poor turnout of crowds on a recent diplomatic trip to South America.[14] There was never any suggestion that Johnson had authorized or even known of the assassination plan, but after the *Chicago Tribune* had published its article the CIA confirmed that it had been contacted by 'foreigners' interested in enlisting the Agency's help in their plot. It certainly bears a hallmark of CIA plots of the 1960s: the assassin, wearing a toxin-laced ring, was to approach a president fatigued from hours of greeting French veterans. He was to shake de Gaulle's hand and then slip into the crowd while the poison did its work.

As confidence in the US government plummeted in the 1970s, the CIA's cloak-and-dagger enterprises of the previous two decades began to look increasingly shabby. What might have appeared a sign of America's advanced technology and superior intelligence resources in the 1950s was now a source of shame. Did a nation that prided itself on its founding principles of democracy and freedom want to be associated with such underhand practices? In early 1975, the Rockefeller Commission began to look into US involvement in foreign assassination plots. By the summer of 1975, the Senate Select Committee to Study Governmental Operations with Respect to Intelligence Activities (known as the Church Committee) had taken over the investigation at the request of President Gerald Ford. He was adamant that political assassination had no part to play in US foreign affairs: 'This administration has not and will not use such means as instruments of foreign policy.'[15] The investigation lasted several months and involved thousands of documents, tens of thousands of sworn testimonies, over one hundred witnesses and sixty days of formal sittings. In the introduction to the committee's findings, Senator

Frank Church described the reason for the investigation, citing truth to its electorate as the basis of America's democracy. The Church Report, as it became known, was an attempt to come clean, to set the murky record straight and, in so doing, to claw back any last shreds of respect that remained in a post-Watergate world. 'The public is entitled to know what the instrumentalities of their government have done … We believe that the truth about the assassination charges should be told because our democracy depends on an informed electorate. Truth is the very anchor of our democracy.'[16]

The 346-page report investigated American involvement in the plots against Patrice Lumumba, Fidel Castro, Rafael Trujillo, Ngo Dinh Diem, Ngo Dinh Nhu and General Rene Schneider of Chile. Its investigation focused on four main questions: (1) whether the United States instigated foreign assassination plots; (2) whether US officials aided foreign dissidents in such a way as to contribute to the killing of foreign leaders; (3) whether such activities were authorized and, if so, at what level of government; and (4) if these activities were not authorized, whether those taking part felt they were within the 'scope of lawful authority', and 'did higher authorities exercise adequate control to prevent such misinterpretation'.[17] This last question, crucially, introduced the issue of accountability and shone a spotlight on the CIA's conscious use of obfuscating language, particularly during the Eisenhower and Johnson administrations.

The investigation concluded that the US government had indeed plotted to kill Patrice Lumumba, but since it had been overtaken by events it did not ultimately bear responsibility for his death. In the case of Castro, the committee found that the US government 'initiated and participated in a series of plots' to kill not only him, but also his brother Raúl and Che Guevara, 'if the opportunity arose'.[18] American culpability in the plots against Rafael Trujillo and Rene Schneider were arguably less clear-cut, but nonetheless allowed the committee to raise questions about the morality of certain American policies. The US government had clearly supplied weapons to Trujillo's enemies in the Dominican Republic with the aim of bringing about an end to his regime, but it had not, however, been directly responsible for his assassination. Nor did the committee find that any US official had been involved in plans to assassinate Schneider. However, the US government had offered support to dissidents plotting his kidnapping, with what the report described as 'certain high officials' aware that Schneider's death was highly likely to follow.

Once the committee was confident of its findings, it investigated how far each president had been involved in the CIA's activities: whether

Senator Frank Church, chairman of the Senate Intelligence Committee, displays a poison dart gun during its investigation into US Intelligence activities, 17 September 1975.

overtly, through direct orders; through veiled language and innuendo (what the report called 'circumlocution' and 'euphemism'); or by turning a blind eye. The last possibility – that the president may have been unaware of CIA activities at the time – was not ruled out, but threw up a completely separate set of problems. Was it better to have a president who was complicit in the CIA's dirty tricks, or was it better to admit that the Agency was, in the committee's memorable words, a 'rogue elephant', accountable to no one and meting out a kind of frontier justice to the rest of the world? In some instances it transpired that not only were the highest officials kept in the dark, but that even within the CIA agents were acting without the knowledge of their director.[19] With confidence in the US government already at an all-time low in the wake of Watergate, the CIA's covert activities were increasingly viewed as a source of embarrassment.

Having investigated US culpability and levels of official accountability, the committee began to question motive. Was there a case for assassination as a defence strategy? Its findings were forthright: none of the plots could be justified in terms of potential danger to the United

States. Only Castro came close to posing any kind of threat, and that was only during the brief period of the Cuban Missile Crisis. But, more significantly, the report's conclusion emphasized the immorality of such attitudes, stressing that the tactics of 'totalitarians' were not a benchmark for US policy: 'Our standards must be higher, and this difference is what the struggle is about. Of course we must defend our democracy. But in defending it, we must resist undermining the very virtues we are defending.'[20] Equally importantly, the committee judged that such tactics could not remain hidden from the world forever, and that, when they became known, they caused 'incalculable' harm to the reputation of the United States government both at home and abroad. The report concluded that 'the undermining of the American public's confidence in its government … is the most damaging consequence of all.'

In 1975, the same year the Select Committee was investigating intelligence activities, further allegations of the Agency's dirty tricks were made public by CIA-defector Philip Agee, whose book *Inside the Company* alleged an even greater US involvement in Latin American affairs than the Church Report had revealed. Its catalogue of CIA plots is familiarly surreal, with references to the use of invisible ink, itching powder, and tranquilized meat to knock out security dogs. It was bad enough that the 'rogue elephant' was trampling upon concepts of democracy and morality; now it appeared to have been scripted by Loony Tunes.

In mitigation, one of the testimonies heard during the Senate Committee was from an FBI official, William C. Sullivan, who described the mindset of a generation of intelligence officers that had been turned 'topsy-turvy during the war'[21] in the attempt to defeat Nazi Germany. The Office of Strategic Strategies (OSS) – the intelligence organization set up during World War II and the CIA's precursor – had been aware of, and to varying degrees involved in, the German Resistance's fight against Hitler. Former CIA director Allen Dulles, for instance, had worked for the OSS out of Switzerland, and papers held at Princeton University reveal that the United States had some prior knowledge of the failed 20 July plot against Hitler.

Sullivan implied that, in times of war, definitions of morality and legality become so loose as to be irrelevant. This view seemed to be backed up by revelations in July 1998 that Britain's Special Operations Executive (SOE) had been involved in its own assassination plot against Hitler, known as Operation Foxley. It never developed beyond the planning stage, and from the outset was beset with difficulties. These were less to do with the plot's moral rights and wrongs than simple doubts over whether it would work. It was felt that assassination attempts might be counterproductive, possibly creating a martyr out of Hitler and bringing about a swell in support like never before. But underlying these questions was the assumption that the Nazi war machine was more than just one man; that the removal of Hitler alone would not be sufficient to stop it. Churchill's speech to the House of Commons on 2 August 1944 reminded the United Kingdom that it should not be relying on assassination plots; instead he invited it to 'put our trust … in our own strong arms and the justice of our cause'.[22]

It was this wartime mentality that seemed to persist within US intelligence networks. A 1954 document advising President Eisenhower on covert activities stated that, in response to threats from abroad, the United States would be justified in employing tactics 'more ruthless than [those] employed by the enemy'. An inevitable casualty of such a strategy, the report advised, was that 'long-standing American concepts of American fair play must be reconsidered'.[23]

From 1976, when the Church Report was issued, the administrations of Gerald Ford and his successor Jimmy Carter remained committed to the principle that assassination had no part to play in US foreign policy. Yet the policies of subsequent administrations were very much dependent on America's sense of its own security. In 1985, Dean Rusk, former secretary of state under presidents Kennedy and Johnson, acknowledged the likely infringement of freedoms in the face of national security threats, stating that 'If a president received what he thought was reliable information that a suitcase containing a nuclear bomb had been hidden away in an American city, our constitutional provisions with respect to search and seizure, and wiretapping, and all our freedoms would go out the window.'[24] The Church Report concluded similarly, stating, 'it is unwise policy to plan or encourage the killing of foreign leaders except under wartime conditions.'[25] This was borne out in 1991: despite General Norman Schwarzkopf's repeated insistence that the United States had no 'policy of trying to kill any particular individual',[26] President George H. W. Bush admitted that, although Saddam Hussein had not been specifically targeted, 'no one will weep for him when he is gone'.[27] In the post-9/11 world, with American vigilance against terrorist threats and the concern for national security at their highest levels since World War II, CIA activities will once again be subject to less scrutiny. According to a senior official under George W. Bush's administration, 'lethal operations that were unthinkable pre-September 11 are now underway'.[28] The fluid morality of assassination was acknowledged by Voltaire two centuries ago: 'Every murderer is punished, unless he kills … to the sound of trumpets.'[29]

Conclusion: *Nationalism and Fundamentalism in the 21st Century*

The case studies in this book were chosen because they embody some of the most important motives and methodologies underlying the practice of assassination, starting with the birth of the concept of political murder through to the state-sanctioned plots of the late 20th century. Using these examples, it is possible to trace how ideas about the justification and legitimacy of assassination have changed, from the ancient philosophical debates on legitimate tyrannicide, to the anarchists' indiscriminate murder of anonymous bystanders, to the 20th-century notion of the crazed, lone gunman.

In the West, one noticeable shift of the last half-century is that political leaders are so isolated from their publics by ranks of impenetrable security that it is nigh-on impossible for the would-be assassin to encroach on the personal space of their head of state: no longer can a modern-day Leon Czolgosz approach the president on the pretext of shaking his hand. The security measures thought necessary to ward off the threat of assassination mean that political leaders appear ever more removed from their electorate, except through the feigned intimacy of television broadcasts and carefully stage-managed events. The assassin is no longer connected to his or her victim by physical proximity, but can nonetheless kill from a distance. After Kennedy's murder, the idea of a president travelling in anything other than a heavily armoured vehicle became inconceivable. There was a collective holding of breath when President Obama defied convention by walking part of the route to the White House during the inaugural ceremonies on 20 January 2009 – the sad but natural response of a world desensitized by acts of violence broadcast on television. The huge growth in mass media that has taken place since the assassination of John F. Kennedy has also given the assassin, or would-be assassin, a worldwide platform on which to air his or her grievances in a way that was unknown in previous centuries.

Although a certain notoriety – if not a warped celebrity – for the assassin are a consequence of a media-saturated society, thus adding a new twist to the story, the methods of and motivations for political killing are essentially a continuation of those already familiar in the late

Benazir Bhutto greets the crowds from a vehicle seconds before a bomb attack that killed her and at least fifteen bystanders. She was returning from a campaign rally in Rawalpindi on 27 December 2007, two weeks before the planned Pakistani general election. Targeted assassination has become a feature of modern terrorist warfare.

above *Indian schoolchildren light candles before an image of Indira Gandhi in 2008, on the twenty-fourth anniversary of the prime minister's death. She was shot by her bodyguards, Sikh extremists, in retaliation for the storming of the Golden Temple in Amritsar, in which Sikh separatists had taken refuge.*

opposite *Mahatma Gandhi with Viscount Mountbatten, the new viceroy of India, and his wife, Edwina, in 1947. Gandhi's philosophy of peaceful resistance brought about the end of British rule in India that year. The following year, Gandhi was shot at point-blank range and killed during evening prayer by Nathuram Godse, who felt Gandhi had betrayed the Hindu cause.*

19th century. Even then, assassins had begun to choose their victims not just for what they did, but also for what they represented – sometimes *only* for what they represented. As though they recognized Cicero's complaint that tyranny continues even when the tyrant is gone, 19th-century assassins increasingly chose their targets for their symbolic value. This allowed them to call attention to specific grievances or ideologies but did not in itself bring about a change in the underlying political system. Gavrilo Princip and his co-conspirators targeted Archduke Franz Ferdinand to draw attention to the Serb nationalist cause, but the absence of the archduke would not in itself help their demands to be met. The depersonalized nature of assassination became entrenched with the rise of anarchism in the 19th century. Just as anarchists targeted political figures for their symbolic value, so symbols themselves were targeted: first institutions that represented the establishment, such as banks and stock exchanges, then symbols of society at large, such as theatres and cafés. The victims of these attacks

right *General Juvénal Habyarimana, president of Rwanda, whose death in a plane crash on 6 April 1994 fanned the flames of civil war and led to genocide. The plane was shot down on its approach into Kigali airport.*

opposite *A Rwanda Patriotic Front (RPF) rebel walks past the site of President Habyarimana's plane crash. The circumstances surrounding the attack — and the identity of its perpetrators — remain unclear.*

were nameless passers-by; the assassin had no grudge against them as individuals, but as abstract symbols of a system they detested.

In the last half-century the idea of targeted terrorism and its accompanying war of propaganda have become central to many nationalist and fundamentalist struggles. From Israel and Palestine to Ireland and the Basque region, and from Africa to the Indian subcontinent, the killing of individual political victims together with the repertoire of mass, indiscriminate death have become all too commonplace aspects of modern politics. Both attempts on Benazir Bhutto's life, for example, involved suicide bombing, with over 160 bystanders killed. In the days following Bhutto's death, on 27 December 2007, al-Qaeda claimed responsibility. Bhutto's assassination is just one in recent years to illustrate that how the assassin and his (or, occasionally, her) victims are represented is central to the political struggle. The figure of the suicide bomber in particular has prompted a rethinking of the idea of the assassin, and the idea of martyrdom is now inextricably linked with political violence. From the perspective of the suicide bomber, piety and righteousness are set against the corrupt and materialistic West, with

heaven as the ultimate award for the sacrificial assassin. To those on the other side of the ideological divide, the suicide bomber symbolizes a terrifying level of fanaticism. What can be done to withstand a threat that doesn't fear its own annihilation but glories in it?

Several recent studies have applied statistical analysis to assassinations, considering which are the most dangerous times and places to be a head of state. In his comprehensive study of political murder,[1] Franklin L. Ford looks at how the number of assassinations diminishes during times of war but rises again in the period immediately afterwards, when a country is in a state of civil discord. The report on assassination and political violence, commissioned by President Johnson in 1968 in the wake of the assassinations of Martin Luther King, Jr., and Robert F. Kennedy, ultimately concluded that the United States' high rate of assassination and assassination attempts is attributable to its particular history. The frontier spirit that is so much a part of America's national identity also has a dark side (the figure of the vigilante, for instance) that legitimizes violence as a means of achieving personal aims.[2] The United Kingdom, on the other hand, has seen only one assassination of a prime minister: Spencer Perceval, who was shot in 1812. In this case, political violence is experienced in the form of terrorism rather than the assassination of the individual; the IRA's attempt on the life of Margaret Thatcher in 1984 was part of a wider terrorist campaign.

In the 21st century, following the September 11 attacks, murder as a political weapon has acquired a whole different meaning. The committing of terrorist atrocities has largely taken over from the targeting of individuals, which itself indicates a shift from a belief in the power of the individual to a belief in collective power. Osama bin Laden's fatwa in 1996 against all Americans is a sinister twist on the 19th-century tradition of aiming at the random public. By singling out ordinary Americans, the implication was that they were responsible for, and ultimately as culpable as, their democratically elected leaders.

The attacks on the World Trade Center have prompted a further reassessment of state involvement in assassination plots. Previously, following the revelations about the illegal activities of the CIA that

Hermann Göring and Martin Bormann visit Hitler's headquarters, the Wolfsschanze, near Rastenburg in East Prussia, in the aftermath of the assassination plot of 20 July 1944. Over 7,000 people were arrested.

OTHER HANDS WILL TAKE UP THE WEAPONS

ICAP

emerged during the Watergate hearings in 1973, a consensus emerged within the US government that the assassination of foreign leaders was not the kind of activity in which a modern, liberal state should be engaged. But in the post-9/11 climate the possibility of 'surgical strikes' against potential terrorists and heads of state has once again returned to the agenda.

One question remains, however: does assassination work? Clearly, some people believe it does, or politically motivated killings would be a thing of the past. Counterfactual history – the 'what if' school of thought – finds endless inspiration in imagining what the world would be like if the attempts against Hitler been successful or the assassination of Kennedy a failure. As an intellectual exercise assassination is compelling, but its fundamental premise – that the whole, elaborate structure of the state depends on one individual – is a fallacy. In some respects it is almost comforting – for the dispossessed especially – to think that a single moment, the time it takes to pull a trigger, to detonate a bomb or to administer a fatal toxin, is all that is needed to right a wrong and alter the course of history. Past events have proven time and time again that this notion is illusory, yet as long as it persists, so will assassination.

Notes

Introduction (pp. 6–13)

1 Speech to the House of Commons, quoted in the *Illustrated London News*, 6 May 1865.

2 From the *Policraticus* (1159), cited in Richard H. Rouse and Mary A. Rouse, 'John of Salisbury and the Doctrine of Tyrannicide', *Speculum* 42:4 (October 1967), p. 695.

Chapter 1 (pp. 14–31)

1 Plutarch, *Life of Caesar*, available online at http://penelope.uchicago.edu/Thayer/E/Roman/Texts/Plutarch/Lives/Caesar*.html (accessed 11 Nov. 2008).

2 The North African prince Jugurtha, cited in David C. Green, *Julius Caesar and its Source* (Salzburg: Universität Salzburg, Institut für Anglistik und Amerikanistik, 1979), p. 2.

3 Cicero, *De Officiis*, Book III, X, available online at http://www.constitution.org/rom/de_officiis.htm#book3 (accessed 11 Nov. 2008); cited in Jane DeRose Evans, *The Art of Persuasion: Political Propaganda from Aeneas to Brutus* (Ann Arbor, Mich.: University of Michigan Press, 1992), p. 90.

4 Plutarch, *Life of Brutus*, available online at http://penelope.uchicago.edu/Thayer/E/Roman/Texts/Plutarch/Lives/Brutus*.html (accessed 11 Nov. 2008).

5 Ibid.

6 Plutarch, *Life of Caesar*.

7 Ibid.

8 Cicero, letter to Atticus XIV.9, cited in Finley Hooper and Matthew Schwartz, *Roman Letters: History from a Personal Point of View* (Detroit: Wayne State University Press, 1991), p. 47.

9 Greg Woolf, *Et Tu, Brute? The Murder of Caesar and Political Assassination* (London: Profile Books, 2006), p. 95.

10 Plutarch, *Life of Caesar*.

11 Cited in Robert A. Lauer, *Tyrannicide and Drama* (Stuttgart: Franz Steiner Verlag, 1987), p. 26.

Chapter 2 (pp. 32–51)

1 Edward Grim, cited in Thomas M. Jones, *The Becket Controversy* (New York and London: John Wiley and Sons, 1970), pp. 55, 56.

2 From the *Thomas Saga*, cited in Michael Staunton, *The Lives of Thomas Becket* (Manchester: Manchester University Press, 2001), p. 42. The *Thomas Saga* is an Icelandic text written in the 14th century, and is an example of the hagiographic treatment that continued for centuries after Becket's death.

3 See Staunton.

4 Roger of Pontigny, cited in Richard Winston, *Thomas Becket* (London: Constable, 1967), p. 125.

5 Ibid., p. 126.

6 Gilbert Foliot, cited in Staunton, p. 21.

7 Cited in M. D. Knowles, *Archbishop Thomas Beckett: A Character Study* (London: British Academy and Oxford University Press, 1949), p. 19.

8 Cited in Winston, p. 303.

9 Henry II's actual words referring to Becket have been variously reported as 'troublesome', 'turbulent', 'meddlesome' and 'low-born'.

10 Cited in Staunton, p. 192.

11 Cited in Winston, p. 343.

12 Edward Grim, cited in Staunton, p. 200.

13 Ibid., p. 201.

14 John Butler, *The Quest for Becket's Bones: The Mystery of the Relics of St Thomas Becket of Canterbury* (New Haven and London: Yale University Press, 1995), p. 25.

15 Cited in Winston, p. 368.

16 See Owen Flanagan, *Varieties of Moral Personality: Ethics and Psychological Realism* (Cambridge, Mass.: Harvard University Press, 1991).

17 John Hudson, Professor of History at St Andrew's University, cited in relation to the BBC's 2006 'Worst Briton' poll. See http://news.bbc.co.uk/1/hi/uk/4663032.stm 9 (accessed 30 Mar. 2009).

Chapter 3 (pp. 52–71)

1 Roland Mousnier, *The Assassination of Henry IV: The Tyrannicide Problem and the Consolidation of the French Absolute Monarchy in the Early Seventeenth Century* (New York: Scribner, 1973), p. 23; originally in Pierre de Lestoile, *Registre-journal*, ed. J. F. Michaud and B. Poujoulat, 2nd series, 1878, p. 587.

2 Robert J. Knecht, *The Rise and Fall of Renaissance France: 1483–1610* (London: Fontana, 1996), p. 567.

3 Ronald S. Love, *Blood and Religion: The Conscience of Henri IV* (Montreal: McGill-Queen's University Press, 2001), p. 302.

4 Ibid.

5 Anita Walker and Edmund H. Dickerman, 'Mind of an Assassin: Ravaillac and the Murder of Henry IV of France', *Canadian Journal of History*, August 1995, p. 11.

6 Ibid., p. 1.

7 Ibid.

8 Mousnier, p. 28.

9 Ibid., p. 50.

10 Ibid.

11 Ibid., p. 51.

Chapter 4 (pp. 72–91)

1 *Le Moniteur Universelle*, 18 July 1793, quoted in Vaughan William and Helen Weston (eds), *Jacques-Louis David's Marat* (Cambridge: Cambridge University Press, 2000), p. 4.

2 Letter to the president of the National Assembly, 1790, quoted in Clifford D. Conner, *Jean-Paul Marat: Scientist and Revolutionary* (Atlantic Highlands, N.J.: Humanities Press, 1998), p. 147.

3 *Offrande à la partrie*, p. 31, quoted in Conner, p. 150.

4 Ibid.

5 Simon Schama, *Citizens* (London: Viking, 1989), p. 734.

6 Quoted in Noel Parker, *Portrayals of Revolution: Images, Debates, and Patterns of Thought on the French Revolution* (New York: Harvester Wheatsheaf, 1990), p. 17.

7 Placard, 'C'en est fait de nous', quoted in Conner, p. 180.

8 *L'Ami du peuple*, 19 August 1792, quoted in Louis R. Gottschalk, *Jean-Paul Marat: A Study in Radicalism* (Chicago: University of Chicago Press, 1967), p. 124.

9 Gottschalk, p. 176, quoting Fabre d'Eglantine.

10 Gottschalk, p. 182.

11 *Société des Jacobins: Recueil de documents*, ed. Alphonse Aulard, 6 volumes (Paris, 1889–97), quoted in Conner, p. 243.

12 Quoted in Conner, p. 246.

13 Thomas Carlyle, *The French Revolution: A History*, III.IV.1, available online at http://www.classicreader.com/read.php/bookid.106/sec.130 (accessed 21 Apr. 2008).

14 Quoted in Schama, p. 741.

15 *The Times*, 10 August 1793, available online at http://www.english.ucsb.edu/faculty/ayliu/research/around-1800/FR/times-8-10-1793.html (accessed 5 Sept. 2008).

Chapter 5 (pp. 92–111)

1 There are several accounts of the number and sequence of cars in the procession, some of which are contradictory. The current information is derived from Luigi Albertini's exhaustive *The Origins of the War of 1914*, tr. and ed. Isabella M. Massey, vol. 2 (Oxford: Oxford University Press, 1953).

2 Albertini, p. 36.

3 Ibid.

4 The seven main conspirators were: Muhamed Mehmedbašić (27 years old); Vaso Čubrilović (17 years old); Nedeljko Čabrinović (19 years old); Cvijetko Popovič (18 years old); Danilo Ilić (24 years old; he was accused of organizing the plot but was not considered a perpetrator); Trifko Grabež (19 years old); and Gavrilo Princip (born 1894; 'not yet twenty').

5 Albertini, p. 45.

6 James Joll, *The Anarchists* (London: Eyre & Spottiswoode, 1964), p. 127.

7 Albertini, p. 21.

8 Ibid., p. 93.

9 Quoted in Franklin L. Ford, *Political Murder: From Tyrannicide to Terrorism* (Cambridge, Mass.: Harvard University Press, 1985), pp. 225–26.

10 Ibid.

11 Ibid., p. 95.

12 Joll, p. 130.

13 Albertini, p. 4.

14 Albertini, p. 5.

Chapter 6 (*pp. 112–31*)

1 Friedrich Katz, *The Life and Times of Pancho Villa* (Stanford, Calif.: Stanford University Press, 1998), p. 790.

2 Rosa King, an Englishwoman who ran a hotel in Morelo's capital, Cuernavaca. Quoted in Roger Parkinson, *Zapata: A Biography* (New York: Stein and Day, 1975), p. 80.

3 Frank McLynn, *Villa and Zapata: A History of the Mexican Revolution* (New York: Carroll & Graf, 2001), p. 277.

4 Ibid., p. 319.

Chapter 7 (*pp. 132–55*)

1 Transcript of Dallas police channels for 22 November 1963, vol. XVII, p. 397, cited in Gerald Posner, *Case Closed* (New York: Random House, 1993), p. 247.

2 Howard Brennan and J. Edward Cherryholmes, *Eyewitness to History: The Kennedy Assassination as Seen by Howard Brennan* (Waco, Tex: Texan Press, 1987), also available at http://www.jfk-online.com/brennan.html, or http://www.jfk-assassination.de/warren/wch/index.php (both accessed 29 Apr. 2008); cited in Posner, p. 246.

3 Warren Commission Report, vol. 7, p. 571, available at http://www.jfk-assassination.de/warren/wch/vol7/page571.php (accessed 29 Apr. 2008).

4 Warren Commission Report, vol. 5, pp. 198–99.

5 David M. Lubin, *Shooting Kennedy: JFK and the Culture of Images* (Berkeley, Calif.: University of California Press, 2003), p. 253.

6 Peter Knight, *The Kennedy Assassination* (Edinburgh: Edinburgh University Press, 2007), p. 44, citing US House of Representatives Select Committee on Assassinations (HSCA), *Investigation of the Assassination of President John F. Kennedy: Hearings* (Washington, D.C.: Government Printing Office, 1979), vol. 3, p. 567.

7 Quoted in Knight, p. 42.

8 William Manchester, *The Death of a President* (London: World Books, 1968), p. 455.

9 See Knight, p. 97.

10 Quoted in Knight, p. 135.

11 Dale Myers's computer-generated footage was aired on America's ABC television channel in November 2003.

Chapter 8 (*pp. 156–73*)

1 These findings were reported in *Interim Report: Alleged Assassination Plots Involving Foreign Leaders*, one of the fourteen reports published by the Church Committee (named after its chairman, Senator Frank Church) between 1975 and 1976. The committee's conclusions led to debates in Congress and, in some cases, to reform. This chapter refers specifically to the report on alleged assassination plots, commonly known as the Church Report.

2 Rhodri Jeffreys-Jones, *The CIA and American Democracy* (New Haven and London: Yale University Press, 1989), p. 97, quoting J. C. King, head of the CIA's Western Hemisphere division.

3 'CIA Plot to Kill Castro Detailed', *Washington Post*, 27 June 2007.

4 US Government Select Committee, *Alleged Assassination Plots Involving Foreign Leaders* (New York: W. W. Norton, 1976), p. 92.

5 Franklin L. Ford, *Political Murder: From Tyrannicide to Terrorism* (Cambridge, Mass.: Harvard University Press, 1985), pp. 378–79.

6 Jeffreys-Jones, p. 97, quoting from *Alleged Assassination Plots*.

7 *Alleged Assassination Plots*, p. 259.

8 Ibid.

9 Ford, p. 327.

10 General Mobutu in 1966, quoted in Ford, p. 327.

11 Ford, p. 379.

12 Jeffreys-Jones, p. 140.

13 *Chicago Tribune*, 15 June 1975, quoted in William Blum, *The CIA, A Forgotten History: U.S. Global Interventions Since World War 2* (London: Zed Books, 1986), p. 169.

14 Blum, p. 169.

15 *Alleged Assassination Plots*, p. xv.

16 Ibid., p. xiii.

17 Ibid., p. xv.

18 Ibid., p. xvi.

19 Loch K. Johnson, *America's Secret Power: The CIA in a Democratic Society* (Oxford and New York: Oxford University Press, 1989), p. 73.

20 *Alleged Assassination Plots*, p. 258.

21 Johnson, p. 250.

22 Quoted in *Operation Foxley: The British Plan to Kill Hitler*, introduction by Mark Seaman, foreword by Ian Kershaw (Richmond, Surrey. Public Record Office, 1998), p. 31.

23 Quoted in Loch K. Johnson, 'Congressional Supervision of America's Secret Agencies: The Experience and Legacy of the Church Committee', in *Public Administration Review* 64:1, pp. 3–14, published online 7 January 2004; originally US Congress. Senate. Select Committee to Study Governmental Operations with Respect to Intelligence Activities (Church Committee). *Final Report*. 95th Cong., 1st sess., May 1976. S. Rept. 94-755, p. 9.

24 Johnson, p. 250.

25 *Alleged Assassination Plots*, p. xxix.

26 Canestaro, Nathan, 'American Law and Policy on Assassinations of Foreign Leaders: The Practicality of Maintaining the Status Quo', *Boston College International and Comparative Law Review* 25:1 (2003), p. 27.

27 Ibid.

28 Ibid., p. 30.

29 Voltaire, *Dictionnaire Philosophique* [1764] (Paris: Imprimerie de Cosse et de Gaultier-Laguionie, 1838), p. 38.

Conclusion (*pp. 174–81*)

1 Franklin L. Ford, *Political Murder: From Tyrannicide to Terrorism* (Cambridge, Mass.: Harvard University Press, 1985).

2 See Peter Knight, *The Kennedy Assassination* (Edinburgh: Edinburgh University Press, 2007).

Further Reading

General

Bell, J. Bowyer, *Assassin: Theory and Practice of Political Violence* (New Brunswick, N.J., and London: Transaction, 2005)

Elliott, Paul, *Assassin! The Bloody History of Political Murder* (London: Blandford, 1999)

Ford, Franklin L., *Political Murder: From Tyrannicide to Terrorism* (Cambridge, Mass.: Harvard University Press, 1985)

Hollingworth, Kris, *How to Kill: The Definitive Story of the Assassin* (London: Century, 2007)

Jardine, Lisa, *The Awful End of Prince William the Silent: The First Assassination of a Head of State with a Hand-gun* (London: HarperCollins, 2005)

Lewis, Bernard, *The Assassins: A Radical Sect in Islam* (London: Weidenfeld and Nicholson, 1967)

Sifakis, Carl, *Encyclopedia of Assassinations* (New York: Facts on File, 1991)

Chapter 1

Armstrong, W. A., 'The Elizabethan Conception of the Tyrant', *The Review of English Studies*, 22:87 (July 1946), pp. 161–81; available online at http://www.jstor.org/stable/508913, (accessed 22 Oct. 2008)

Cicero, *De Officiis*, Book III, X, available online at http://www.constitution.org/rom/de_officiis.htm#book3 (accessed 11 Nov. 2008)

Clarke, M. L., *The Noblest Roman: Marcus Brutus and his Reputation* (London: Thames & Hudson, 1981)

Dean, Leonard F. (ed.), *Twentieth Century Interpretations of Julius Caesar: A Collection of Critical Essays* (Englewood Cliffs, N.J.: Prentice-Hall, 1968)

Evans, Jane DeRose, *The Art of Persuasion: Political Propaganda from Aeneas to Brutus* (Ann Arbor, Mich.: University of Michigan Press, 1992)

Froude, James Anthony, *Caesar: A Sketch* (London: Longmans, Green and Co., 1890)

Fuller, J. F. C., *Julius Caesar: Man, Soldier and Tyrant* (London: Eyre and Spottiswood, 1965)

Gelzer, Matthias, *Caesar: Politician and Statesman*, tr. Peter Needham (Cambridge, Mass.: Harvard University Press, 1968)

Girard, René, *Collective Violence and Sacrifice in Shakespeare's Julius Caesar*, Bennington Chapbooks in Literature (Bennington, Va.: Bennington College, 1990)

Green, David C., *Julius Caesar and its Source* (Salzburg: Universität Salzburg, Institut für Anglistik und Amerikanistik, 1979)

Hooper, Finlay, and Matthew Shwartz, *Roman Letters: History from a Personal Point of View* (Detroit: Wayne State University Press, 1991)

Lauer, Robert A., *Tyrannicide and Drama* (Stuttgart: Franz Steiner Verlag, 1987)

Meier, Christian, *Caesar*, tr. David McLintock (London: Fontana Press, 1982)

Plutarch, *Life of Brutus*, available online at http://penelope.uchicago.edu/Thayer/E/Roman/Texts/Plutarch/Lives/Brutus*.html (accessed 11 Nov. 2008)

Plutarch, *Life of Caesar*, available online at http://penelope.uchicago.edu/Thayer/E/Roman/Texts/Plutarch/Lives/Caesar*.html (accessed 11 Nov. 2008)

Shakespeare, William, *Julius Caesar* (London: Penguin Classics, 2005)

Suetonius, *The Twelve Caesars*, available online at http://ancienthistory.about.com/library/bl/bl_text_suetcaesar.htm (accessed 11 Nov. 2008)

Vivian, Thomas, *Julius Caesar* (Hemel Hempstead: Harvester Wheatsheaf, 1992)

Woolf, Greg, *Et Tu, Brute? The Murder of Caesar and Political Assassination* (London: Profile Books, 2006)

Chapter 2

Alexander, James W., 'The Becket Controversy in Recent Historiography', *The Journal of British Studies*, 9:2 (May 1970), pp. 1–26

Anouilh, Jean, *Becket ou L'Honneur de Dieu* (Paris: La Table Ronde, 1959)

Aubé, Pierre, *Thomas Becket* (Paris: Editions Fayard, 1988)

Barlow, Frank, *Thomas Becket* (London: Weidenfeld and Nicholson, 1986)

Borenius, Tancred, *St Thomas Becket in Art* (London: Methuen, 1932)

Brown, Paul Alonzo, 'The Development of the Legend of Thomas Becket' (PhD thesis, University of Pennsylvania, 1930)

Butler, John, *The Quest for Becket's Bones: The Mystery of the Relics of St Thomas Becket of Canterbury* (New Haven and London: Yale University Press, 1995)

Eliot, T. S., *Murder in the Cathedral* (London: Faber & Faber, 1935)

Holmes, Urban Tigner, *Daily Living in the Twelfth Century: Based on the Observations of Alexander Neckham in London and Paris* (Madison, Wis.: University of Wisconsin Press, 1962)

Jones, Thomas M., *The Becket Controversy* (New York and London: John Wiley and Sons, 1970)

Knowles, M. D., *Archbishop Thomas Beckett: A Character Study* (London: British Academy and Oxford University Press, 1949)

McKenna, J. W., 'Popular Canonization as Political Propaganda: The Cult of Archbishop Scrope', *Speculum* 45:4 (Oct. 1970), pp. 608–23

Robertson, James Craigie, *Becket, Archbishop of Canterbury: A Biography* (London: John Murray, 1859)

Rouse, Richard H., and Mary A. Rouse, 'John of Salisbury and the Doctrine of Tyrannicide', *Speculum* 42:4 (October 1967), pp. 693–709

Scully, Robert E., 'The Unmaking of a Saint: Thomas Becket and the English Reformation', *The Catholic Historical Review*, 86:4 (Oct. 2000), pp. 579–602

Staunton, Michael, *The Lives of Thomas Becket* (Manchester: Manchester University Press, 2001)

Theilmann, John M., 'Medieval Pilgrims and the Origins of Tourism', *The Journal of Popular Culture* 20:4 (Spring 1987), pp. 93–102

——, 'English Peasants and Medieval Miracle Lists', available at http://www.blackwell-synergy.com/doi/pdf/10.1111/j.1540-6563.1990.tb00782.x (accessed 4 June 2008)

Urry, William, *Thomas Becket: His Last Days* (Stroud: Sutton Publishing, 1999)

Williamson, Hugh Ross, *The Arrow and the Sword: An Essay in Detection* (London: Faber & Faber, 1947)

Winston, Richard, *Thomas Becket* (London: Constable, 1967)

Chapter 3

Buisseret, David, *Henry IV: King of France* (New York: Routledge, 1990)

Burke, Peter, *Popular Culture in Early Modern Europe* (New York: Harper & Row, 1978)

Davis, Natalie Zemon, *Society and Culture in Early Modern France* (Stanford, Calif.: Stanford University Press, 1975)

Febvre, Lucien, *Life in Renaissance France*, tr. Marian Rothstein (Cambridge, Mass.: Harvard University Press, 1977)

Greengrass, Mark, *France in the Age of Henri IV: The Struggle for Stability* (London: Longman, 1984)

Holt, Mack P., *The French Wars of Religion: 1562–1629* (Cambridge: Cambridge University Press, 1995)

Hussey, Andrew, *Paris: The Secret History* (London: Penguin, 2007)

Kettering, Sharon, *French Society 1589–1717* (Edinburgh: Pearson Education, 2001)

Knecht, Robert J., *The Rise and Fall of Renaissance France: 1483-1610* (London: Fontana, 1996)

Love, Ronald S., *Blood and Religion: The Conscience of Henri IV* (Montreal: McGill-Queen's University Press)

Mousnier, Roland, *The Assassination of Henry IV: The Tyrannicide Problem and the Consolidation of the French Absolute Monarchy in the Early Seventeenth Century* (New York: Scribner, 1973)

Ranum, Orest, 'The French Ritual of Tyrannicide in the Late Sixteenth Century', *Sixteenth Century Journal* 11:1 (Spring 1980), pp. 63–82

Salmon, J. H. M., 'The Afterlife of Henry of Navarre', *History Today* 47:10 (Oct. 1997), pp. 12–18

Vivanti, Corrado, 'Henry IV, the Gallic Hercules', *Journal of the Warburg and Courtauld Institutes*, 30 (1967), pp. 176–97

Walker, Anita M., and Edmund H. Dickerman, 'Mind of an Assassin: Ravaillac and the Murder of Henry IV of France', *Canadian Journal of History* 30:2 (Aug. 1995), p. 201

Chapter 4

Conner, Clifford D., *Jean-Paul Marat, Scientist and Revolutionary* (Atlantic Highlands, N.J.: Humanities Press, 1998)

Darnton, Robert, and Daniel Roche (eds), *Revolution in Print: The Press in France 1775–1800* (Berkeley, Calif.: University of California Press, 1989)

Doyle, William, *The Oxford History of the French Revolution* (Oxford: Oxford University Press, 2002)

Epois, Jean, *L'Affaire Corday-Marat* (Les Sables-d'Olonne, France: Le Cercle d'or, 1980)

Funck-Brentano, *Marat ou Le Mensonge des mots* (Paris: Editions Bernard Grasset, 1941)

Gelbart, Nina Rattner, 'The Blonding of Charlotte Corday', *Eighteenth-Century Studies* 38:1 (2004), pp. 201–21

Gottschalk, Louis R., *Jean-Paul Marat: A Study in Radicalism* (Chicago: University of Chicago Press, 1967)

Gough, Hugh, *The Newspaper Press in the French Revolution* (London: Routledge, 1988)

Kennedy, Emmet, *A Cultural History of the French Revolution* (New Haven and London: Yale University Press, 1989)

Kindleberger, Elizabeth R., 'Charlotte Corday in Text and Image: A Case Study in the French Revolution and Women's History', *French Historical Studies* 18:4 (Autumn 1994), pp. 969–99

Leith, James A., *The Idea of Art as Propaganda in France 1750–1799: A Study in the History of Ideas* (Toronto: University of Toronto Press, 1965)

Marat, Jean-Paul, *Dénonciation faite au tribunal du public ... contre m. Necker* ([n.p.], c. 1790)

Parker, Noel, *Portrayals of Revolution: Images, Debates, and Patterns of Thought on the French Revolution* (New York: Harvester Wheatsheaf, 1990)

Popkin, Jeremy D., *Revolutionary News: The Press in France 1789–1799* (Durham, N.C.: Duke University Press)

Roche, Daniel, *The People of Paris: An Essay in Popular Culture in the 18th Century*, tr. Marie Evans in assoc. with Gwynne Lewis (Leamington Spa: Berg, 1987)

Rose, R. B., *The Making of the Sans-Culottes: Democratic Ideas and Institutions in Paris, 1789–92* (Manchester: Manchester University Press, 1983)

Schama, Simon, *Citizens* (London: Viking, 1989)

Soboul, Albert, *The Parisian Sans-Culottes and the French Revolution 1793–4* (Oxford: Clarendon Press, 1964)

Vovelle, Michel (ed.), *Marat: Écrits* (Paris: Messidor, 1988)

William, Vaughan, and Helen Weston (eds), *Jacques-Louis David's Marat* (Cambridge: Cambridge University Press, 2000)

Chapter 5

Albertini, Luigi, *The Origins of the War of 1914*, tr. and ed. Isabella M. Massey, vol. 2 (Oxford: Oxford University Press, 1953)

Carter, April, *The Political Theory of Anarchism* (Routledge and Kegan Paul: London, 1971)

Clymer, Jeffory A., *America's Culture of Terrorism: Violence, Capitalism, and the Written Word* (Chapel Hill, N.C.: University of North Carolina Press, 2003)

Elory, Hippolyte, *L'Anarchie* ([Dole], c. 1848); available online at http://galenet.galegroup.com/servlet/MOME?af=RN&ae=U106810263&srchtp=a&ste=14 (accessed Oct. 2008)

Evans, R. J. W., and Hartmut Pogge von

Strandmann (eds), *The Coming of the First World War* (Oxford: Clarendon Press, 1988)

Fleming, D. F., *Origins and Legacies of World War I* (New York: Doubleday, 1968)

Hobsbawm, Eric J., *The Age of Empire* (London: Weidenfeld and Nicholson, 1987)

Joll, James, *The Anarchists* (London: Eyre & Spottiswoode, 1964)

——, *The Origins of the First World War* (London: Longman, 1984; 2nd edn 1992)

Kedward, Roderick, *The Anarchists: The Men Who Shocked an Era* (New York: American Heritage Press, 1971)

MacKenzie, David, *The Serbs and Russian Pan-Slavism 1875–1878* (Ithaca, N.Y.: Cornell University Press, 1967)

Petrovich, Michael Boro, *A History of Modern Serbia 1804–1918*, vol. 2 (New York and London: Harcourt Brace Jovanovich, 1976)

Warner, Philip, *World War One: A Narrative* (London: Cassel Military Classics, 1998)

Chapter 6

Gilbert, Dennis, 'Emiliano Zapata: Textbook Hero', *Mexican Studies / Estudios Mexicanos* 19:1 (Winter 2003), pp. 127–59

Hart, John Mason, *Revolutionary Mexico* (Berkeley, Calif.: University of California Press, 1987)

Katz, Friedrich, 'Pancho Villa and the Attack on Columbus, New Mexico', *The American Historical Review* 83:1 (Feb. 1978), pp. 101–30

——, *The Life and Times of Pancho Villa* (Stanford, Calif.: Stanford University Press, 1998)

Klapp, Orrin E., 'The Folk Hero', *The Journal of American Folklore* 62:243 (Jan.–Mar. 1949), pp. 17–25

Knight, Alan, *The Mexican Revolution*, 2 vols (Cambridge: Cambridge University Press, 1986)

McLynn, Frank, *Villa and Zapata: A History of the Mexican Revolution* (New York: Carroll & Graf, 2001)

Millon, Robert P., *Zapata: The Ideology of a Peasant Revolutionary* (New York: International Publishers, 1969)

O'Malley, Ilene V., *The Myth of the Revolution: Hero Cults and the Institutionalization of the Mexican State* (New York: Greenwood Press, 1986)

Parkinson, Roger, *Zapata: A Biography* (New York: Stein and Day, 1975)

Sandos, James A., 'Pancho Villa and

American Security: Woodrow Wilson's
Mexican Diplomacy Reconsidered',
Journal of Latin American Studies 13:2
(Nov. 1981) pp. 293–311

Womack, John, Jr., *Zapata and the Mexican
Revolution* (New York: Alfred A. Knopf,
1969)

——, 'The Spoils of the Mexican
Revolution', *Foreign Affairs* (July 1970),
pp. 677–87

Chapter 7

Goldbert, Robert Alan, *Enemies Within:
The Culture of Conspiracy in Modern America*
(New Haven and London: Yale
University Press, 2001)

Knight, Peter, *The Kennedy Assassination*
(Edinburgh: Edinburgh University Press,
2007)

—— (ed.), *Conspiracy Theories in American
History: An Encyclopedia* (Santa Barbara,
Calif.: ABC-Clio, 2003)

Lubin, David M., *Shooting Kennedy: JFK and
the Culture of Images* (Berkeley, Calif.:
University of California Press, 2003)

Manchester, William, *The Death of a President*
(London: World Books, 1968)

Posner, Gerald, *Case Closed: Lee Harvey Oswald
and the Assassination of JFK* (New York:
Anchor, 1993)

Rauchway, Eric, *Murdering McKinley:
The Making of Theodore Roosevelt's America*
(New York: Hill and Wang, 2003)

Sondheim, Stephen, and John Weidman,
Assassins (New York: Theater
Communications Group, 1991)

Talbot, David, *Brothers: The Hidden History of
the Kennedy Years* (New York: Simon &
Schuster, 2007)

Chapter 8

Agee, Philip, *Inside the Company: CIA Diary*
(London: Allen Lane), 1975

——, and Louis Wolf, *Dirty Work: The CIA in
Western Europe* (Secaucus, N.J.: Lyle
Stuart, 1978)

Blum, William, *The CIA, A Forgotten History:
U.S. Global Interventions Since World War 2*
(London: Zed Books, 1986)

Canestaro, Nathan, 'American Law and
Policy on Assassinations of Foreign
Leaders: The Practicality of Maintaining
the Status Quo', *Boston College International
and Comparative Law Review* 25:1 (2003);
available online at http://heinonline.org/
HOL/Page?collection=journals&handle
=hein.journals/bcic26&div=6&size=
2&rot=0&type=image (accessed
15 Dec. 2008)

Fest, Joachim, *Plotting Hitler's Death: The
German Resistance to Hitler*, tr. Bruce Little
(London: Weidenfeld and Nicholson,
1996)

Hinckle, Warren, and William W. Turner,
*Deadly Secrets: The CIA–Mafia War Against
Castro and the Assassination of J.F.K.* (New
York: Thunder's Mouth Press, 1992)

Hoffmann, Peter, *The History of the German
Resistance 1933–1945*, tr. Richard Barry
(London: Macdonald and Jane's, 1977)

Jeffreys-Jones, Rhodri, *The CIA and American
Democracy* (New Haven and London:
Yale University Press, 1989)

——, *Cloak and Dollar: A History of American
Secret Intelligence* (New Haven and
London: Yale University Press, second
edition 2002)

Johnson, Loch K., *America's Secret Power:
The CIA in a Democratic Society* (Oxford
and New York: Oxford University Press,
1989)

Operation Foxley: The British Plan to Kill Hitler,
introduction by Mark Seaman, foreword
by Ian Kershaw (Richmond, Surrey:
Public Record Office, 1998)

Rigden, Denis, *Kill the Führer: Section X and
Operation Foxley* (Stroud: Sutton
Publishing, 1999)

US Government Select Committee, *Alleged
Assassination Plots Involving Foreign Leaders.
An Interim Report of the Select Committee to
Study Governmental Operations* (New York:
W. W. Norton, 1976)

List of Illustrations

Index

Page numbers in *italic* refer to illustrations and the content of related captions.